A Living History of

The Middle Ages

The Fall of Rome through the Renaissance

Written and Illustrated by Angela O'Dell

© jellybeanjar PUBLICATIONS™ 2015

A Living History of Our World
The Middle Ages

Written and Illustrated by Angela O'Dell
For all of my young friends who are striving to reach high,
especially the Anderson gang

Soli Deo Gloria

Dave and Angela O'Dell

Table of Contents

Table of Contents

Table of Contents

Table of Contents

Table of Contents

Many thanks to Kyrsten Carlson
for her superior editing skills and her willingness
to help with this book.
You are such a blessing!

Many, many thanks to the Tiffany family for
allowing me to use their pictures on the covers of
this book and the accompanying
Student's Journal.

Introduction

Welcome to <u>A Living History of Our World, The Middle Ages.</u> I hope you enjoy our continued journey through the incredible story of world history.

If you and your family have completed any or all of the volumes in this series, you are already comfortable with the layout and the style of the books. However, for the convenience of all newcomers, I will explain how this course is to be used. The American history volumes in this series were created with a certain age range in mind, but this volume and the other volumes covering world history are written to be used with all ages together.

The history of the world should be learned by all people. As parents, it is our responsibility to our children to make sure that they understand history did not start with Christopher Columbus sailing the ocean blue in 1492. History is much older than that!

<u>"A Living God for Living Education"</u>

Charlotte Mason once said, "<u>The indwelling of Christ is a thought particularly fit for the children, because their large faith does not stumble at the mystery, their imagination leaps readily to the marvel, that the King Himself should inhabit a little child's heart.</u>" God is alive. Not only is He alive now, but He has always been so. Studying world history, through Christian worldview glasses, allows a child to see history for what it truly is - <u>HIS</u>tory.

My goal in writing this curriculum is to make an easy-to-use, comprehensive history resource for you to use with your whole family at one time, with little to no preparation and no necessary supplement. (If you are doing this study as a family, you may even choose to have a journal for each of the parents involved in the study.)

<u>How to use "A Living History of Our World: The Middle Ages"</u>

This curriculum has two parts: this history storybook and the Student's Journal. There are twenty-eight chapters and four built-in reviews, making it quite attainable to finish in one school year. The journal pages are

Introduction

an assortment of areas to write/journal, hands-on projects and pictures to color. There is also a section of timeline projects (instructions included), deeper research topics, and several optional projects.

Unique to the world history volumes in this series, are the reproducible "Student Research" packets included in the back of each Student Journal. There are two packets; one is appropriate for your junior high student, and the other is deep enough for your senior high schooler. Elementary students may simply use the Student Journal pages to record what they are learning, while their older siblings will also use these convenient research forms to dig even deeper into their studies. I have included a list of research tools for these older students that will make their studies more meaningful. In the appendix of this volume, I have included a list of additional research topics for your junior high and high school students. These additional research topics are plentiful and are meant to be assigned by you, the parent/teacher. I would suggest planning on having your junior high student complete one research topic per two weeks, and your senior high student complete three each month. (You make the ultimate decision, though, as you know your children's abilities.)

Your younger children will find everything they need to complete their journal pages in an encyclopedia, or online. By having your children use an encyclopedia a couple times a week, you can easily teach important research skills. Of course, if your children are very small, don't feel like you need to have them do this. Make this curriculum fit your family. For your convenience, I have included a schedule to work through this course. You will find the suggested schedule in the appendix of this book.

Including geography in your study

Many of the lessons have geographical locations in them. Have your globe or world map handy, so that you and your children can find them after you finish reading. You may also want to include simple map reading skills.

Introduction

Just say, "What continent is _____ on?" or "What hemisphere is _____ in?" By simply including this information into your conversation, you familiarize your children with geographical terms.

More on supplementing

Please remember if your younger children do only what is included in this book and in the Student's Journal, you will have done enough! However, I am aware that there are children who love to read and want to know more about a particular historical topic. For these children and for the families who enjoy historical read-alouds, I have included a supplemental book lists in the appendix of this book.

An Important Note on Narration

A Living History of Our World is written in the Charlotte Mason style. Narration is a key element of this curriculum. Please take the time to employ oral narration whenever the book suggests it. Included in the Student's Journal is a section of written narration prompts for the older child.

What preparations do you need to get ready for a wonderful year of history?

1. Have this book for you, as a teacher, and a Student's Journal for each of your children. Junior high and high school students may wish to have their own copy of this book also.

2. Determine how many research topics you want your older students to complete and make the appropriate number of copies of the "Student Research Aids" packet.

3. You will need the following items to complete your Student's Journal:

   ☐ Scissors

   ☐ Glue

Introduction

☐ Colored pencils, markers and crayons

☐ Hole punch

☐ Stapler

☐ Hole re-enforcers

☐ Construction paper

☐ Poster board (optional)

☐ Contact paper

☐ Brass fasteners

☐ Encyclopedias (books or CD ROM)

☐ Old magazines for pictures

☐ World map or globe

☐ Two, 3-ring notebook*** for each of your jr. and sr. high students

☐ One, 3-ring notebook*** for your elementary students

☐ NOTE: 1.5 or 2 inch notebooks with clear plastic sleeve covers work best.

*Please use close parent supervision when young children are using the internet.

*** If you are continuing your journey through world history and have completed The Story of the Ancients in this series, you will want to simply add to the timeline you started in that volume.

Introduction

"We see, then, that the children's lessons should provide material for their mental growth, should exercise the several powers of their minds, should furnish them with fruitful ideas, and should afford them knowledge, really valuable for its own sake, accurate, and interesting, of the kind that the child may recall as a man with profit and pleasure." Charlotte Mason

(The Original Homeschooling Series, Volume 1, Part V Lessons as Instruments of Education, p.177)

All quotes are categorized in the "Works Cited" page in the appendix.

All illustrations and pictures are private property. (Any illustrations not created by the author/illustrator of this book are vector free, royalty free, public domain images.)

Introduction

Chapter 1

The First Century Anno Domini

If you traveled with me through Volume 4 of this series, you will remember how we toured the ancient lands and times, discovering the rise and fall of the many civilizations of that time. Some of these civilizations were small and seemingly unimportant, while others were mighty and flung their influence far and wide throughout the world.

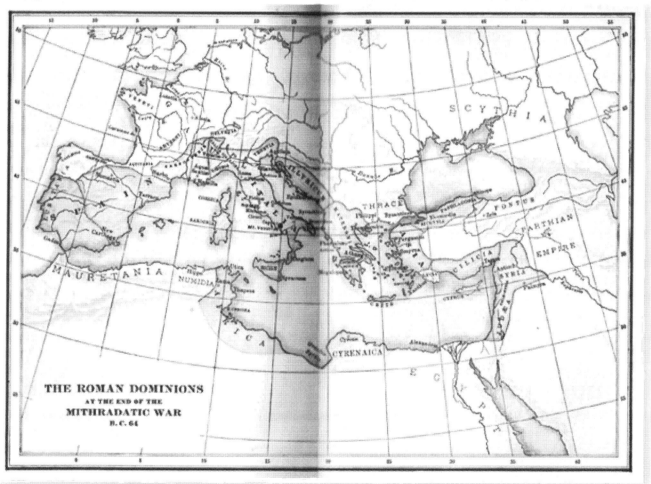

THE ROMAN DOMINIONS
AT THE END OF THE
MITHRADATIC WAR
B.C. 64

At the peak of its power, the Roman Empire covered an enormous area.

We are going to begin this section of our journey through world history by rewinding just a little. In our previous volume, we learned about the mighty

Roman Empire, which became the ruler of the world. The Roman Empire was not only widespread, but its culture was hugely influential on the the rest of the world, becoming the foundation of countless other cultures. Even the Roman government set a pattern for many other governments to follow.

Only the empires of the Orient, China and India were not controlled or influenced greatly by the Roman Empire. These civilizations were secluded and far enough away from the Middle East that they were able to maintain their independence and unique identities throughout the centuries. (In later chapters, we will learn more about these civilizations during the Middle Ages.)

The Roman Empire became so immensely vast, it was impossible for one emperor to control or protect the entire kingdom. "Barbarians" nibbled away at the unprotected edges of the kingdom, weakening the northern borders until the empire was compromised. These people from the north were called "Barbarians" because the civilized world thought of them as uncouth and uncivilized. Their warriors were tough and were known for being quite vicious and cruel. These roving tribes eventually overran the great Roman Empire. In a little while, we will learn about what happened with the Roman Empire and how it affected the world even after its demise, but first, we will take some time to learn about the early Christians.

As we glance back over the years following the crucifixion and resurrection of our Lord and Savior, Jesus Christ, we see the church emerging from the shadows. The friends and followers of Jesus became known as the Apostolic Elders of this early church. At the end of Volume 4, we met these early Christians, who faced incredible persecution from the Roman rulers. Do you remember what they did to escape this persecution? Many of the Roman

Christians went into hiding. They dug massive tunnels and caves, called catacombs, under the city of Rome.

You may be wondering why the Christians were so persecuted. This is a good question! To understand this persecution, we need to discover why the Christians would be viewed as a threat. This is rather puzzling because the Christians were peaceful and, for the most part, model citizens. Many of them were first or second generation followers of Jesus. By this, I mean that many of them had known Christ while He was here on earth as a human. Some of them were the children of the people Jesus had healed. Their leaders were the Apostolic Elders, and later, the ones trained by these elders. These were many of the people who had been saved when the Holy Spirit had come to indwell the disciples after Jesus had died, resurrected, and ascended into Heaven. If you haven't read this story, I encourage you to read it in the book of Acts, chapters 1 and 2.

One of the reasons the Christians were persecuted by many non-believers was because the Roman culture did not understand them. Many Romans rejected the Christians as "atheists" because the Christians refused to worship the many Roman gods. Christianity also challenged the social order of the Roman culture. Who can come to Jesus? Everyone can! This idea puzzled many Romans, and some of them were even threatened by it. If anyone could have a relationship with Jesus Christ and salvation from their sins, then the high ranking social status meant nothing. This angered many people, who caused trouble for the Christians, but it brought hope to countless others.

In spite of, or perhaps because of, this persecution, the early church grew in leaps and bounds during the first several hundred years after Christ.

Sometimes going through difficulty makes believers turn to God more. Perhaps these believers remembered the words of Christ, when He said, "Blessed are they which are persecuted for righteousness' sake: for theirs is the kingdom of heaven. Blessed are ye, when men shall revile you, and persecute you, and shall say all manner of evil against you falsely, for my sake. Rejoice, and be exceeding glad: for great is your reward in heaven: for so persecuted they the prophets which were before you." Matthew 5:10-11

These Christians were a good testimony to their neighbors, and as others saw how the church continued to grow, they wanted to know more about this hope and peace. When we study the contrast between the Roman culture, which did not treat women, children, and slaves with equality, and the beliefs of the Christians, it is no wonder people were attracted to this "new" religion.

In Christianity, everyone is welcome to come to Jesus. The teachings of the apostles showed Christ Himself interacting with women, children, men and even slaves and servants. Christianity granted respect to everyone. The teachings based on the writings of the apostles were also based on love, grace, mercy, and respect. This appealed to those beaten down by the Roman government and culture. Probably the most appealing aspect of Christianity was, and still is, the prospect of having a personal relationship with God. Romans knew that their gods could be "fickle" - pleased with them one moment, and angry the next, and always distant, without the ability to have a relationship with mere mortals. Through the Person of Jesus, it is possible to have a real and living relationship with the God of the Universe.

Narration Break: Talk about why some Romans were insulted by Christianity, while others were drawn to it.

Chapter 1

You may think that, since the early Christians were close to the time of Jesus, they would not have to deal with false teachings. Even at this time, so close to the life of Christ, Christians had to be on guard against heresy. There were those among them teaching what they called "secret knowledge." These teachers claimed to have experienced secret knowledge of God. They believed and taught that Jesus did not really become flesh. Of course, we know that the Bible says that, "the Word became flesh and dwelled among men." These false teachers were called Gnostics (NOS-tics).

The Christians knew they needed to come together and stand up against such false teachings. They trained their young people to know the truth using the Apostolic teachings. They were very careful to measure everything against these teachings. Biblical truth became the foundation for many hymns written during these years.

Hymn written to fight the Gnostic Worldview

"The great Creator of the worlds,
The sovereign God of heav'n,
A holy and immortal truth
To us on earth has giv'n
A holy and immortal truth
To us on earth has giv'n!"

"God sent Christ down as
sending God;
One man for humankind;
As one with us
Christ dwelt with us,
And died and lives on high.
As one with us
Christ dwelt with us,
And died and lives on high!"

"God sent no angel of the host
To bear this might World:
But Christ through whom the worlds
were made
The everlasting Lord.
Yes, Christ through whom the worlds
were made
The everlasting Lord!"
-Epistle of Dognetus

Chapter 1

The Bible was very important to the early Christians, but in fact, the only "Bible" these people had was the Old Testament. The books the apostles had written, as well as the letters from Paul to the churches in Philippi, Corinth, Ephesus, Galatia, and Rome, were also in the possession of the church, but they had not been officially accepted as part of the Bible. These books, along with the books of prophecy at the end of the New Testament, were called the "Canon."

I once thought that this was an odd name for these writings until I learned the story of how it came to be. The word "canon" means "measuring stick." By using this word, the Christians were referring to the books that God had inspired, to form the church's faith. These writings of the Apostolic Elders were called the "canon," because they measured the boundaries of the Christian belief system and protected them against the heresy of false teachers.

We will learn more about how the Bible came to us a little later on in our story. I love how we can always rely on God's Word. The next time you read your Bible, remember, it is a "canon" - a measuring stick for your life!

It was during this first century that a man named Josephus lived (37-100 AD) in the Roman Empire. His alternative names are his Hebrew name, Joseph ben Matityahu and his Roman name, Titus Flavius Josephus. Josephus was a historian, a hagiographer (hay-gee-O-gru-fer), and a rather controversial fellow. This means he wrote about historical events and specialized in recording the happenings of the "Saints*" and ecclesiastical leaders. In other words, he wrote biographies about the important people in the early church. It is because of his writings**, we know a little about what happened in these early years A.D. (Anno Domini).

We can thank Josephus for the accounts of the siege of Masada. If you were with me in Volume 4, you might remember how we learned about the Dead Sea Scrolls, which were found in a cave near the ruins of the Jewish fortress, Masada. Josephus was not the man who wrote those scrolls, but he is the one who described the area in great detail.

Narration Break: <u>What are some ways the Christians fought against false teachings?</u>

* The term "Saint(s)" is used often in this time period to describe revered men or women of the early church. This term does not imply that these people were worshipped in any way.

** The writer, Josephus, is a controversial figure in history. He was born to a Hebrew family, spent years fighting against the Roman occupation, and in his later years, became sympathetic to the Roman government. His writings were scorned by the Christian historic community for years but have recently been found to be mostly accurate.

Chapter 2

A Series of Important Events

Before we move forward with our study of the Middle Ages, I want to tell you about a series of important events, some which happened in Israel after Christ had returned to Heaven. As we have learned, the nation of Israel arose from a family, which God had chosen to be His special people. These would be the people from whom God's own Son would come to set the human race free from their sins. Israel had a long and troubling history punctuated by captivities and deliverances, prophecies and blessings, faithfulness and rebellion.

Hebrew prophecies had foretold the birth of Christ centuries before His birth, but when He came, many did not believe that He was the Messiah. They continued to hold out hope for the prophecies to be fulfilled, even though Christ had come and fulfilled every single prophetic criteria (requirements).

The Romans came and devastated the Jews' country in a war during the years AD 66 - 73. (This is the war that led to the siege of Masada.) When the Roman emperor tried to prevent the Jews from living in Jerusalem, they revolted, and again established an independent state. This revolt, which was known as the bar Kokhba revolt was led by a man named Simon bar Kokhba.

Let's discover why this man is a very interesting figure in history, starting with his name. Simon bar Kokhba was born with the Hebrew name Simon ben Kosiba. The name "bar Kokhba," which means "Son of a Star" in Aramaic, was taken from a prophecy in Numbers 24:17, "There shall step forth a star out of Jacob, and a scepter shall rise out of Israel..." As Christians, we know that the "scepter... out of Israel" was Jesus Christ,

A coin from the time of Bar Kokhba revolt.

but many of the Jews, who were still looking for the Messiah to come, had hope that this man would deliver them from the Romans. At first it appeared that he would be able to keep the Romans out, but the independent state, which bar Kokhba had established, lasted only three, short years before the Romans came in and crushed them again. Israel would not be an independent state again for over a thousand years.

In our last chapter, we talked about how huge the Roman Empire was. We discussed the fact that it was so large, there was no good way to protect it. In fact, the Roman emperor was called the "ruler of the world," but how could one person rule the entire world? The very size of the empire became its downfall. There were many problems plaguing the Roman Empire at this time...including the plague. This terrible sickness killed thousand upon thousands of people, therefore weakening the army. Between the Barbarians chipping away at the borders, sickness, poverty, and bad emperors, the Roman Empire was becoming weaker and weaker.

In AD 284, an emperor, who had a plan to save the empire, came to the throne. Emperor Diocletian decided to split the empire into two parts; he would rule over one part, and he would appoint a co-emperor to rule over the other part. Diocletian appointed himself to be emperor of the Eastern Empire, which included the lands spreading from Egypt in the south, up into Asia Minor in the north. He appointed a man named Maximian to rule the Western Empire, which was made up of the lands around the Mediterranean Sea, including the boot-shaped Italy. Next, he placed two more rulers in place. These two rulers were called Caesars, and their job was to help each emperor rule each part of the divided empire. (This "rule of four" is called a

"Tetrarchy" [TET-rar-key].) Diocletian hoped having four men ruling instead of one would be more efficient, but it was wishful thinking on his part, I'm afraid.

So what do you think happened to the Roman Empire, now ruled by four men instead of one? Have you ever heard the expression, "Too many cooks spoil the soup"? This situation is a good example of what this saying means. The Caesars, Galerius (gu-LAY-re-us) in the Eastern Empire, and Constantius in the Western Empire, came to the throne after Diocletian and Maximian died. These two fellows could not get along because they both wanted to rule the entire empire. Galerius hated the Christians, and horrible persecution broke out againts the Church. The empire was in turmoil; things were not going well at all!

Things went from bad to worse when Galerius kidnapped Constantius' son. It appeared that Galerius was going to get his way after all, when Constantius became gravely ill. Galerius must have been feeling quite certain of his impending victory because he allowed Constantine to go visit his father. It is no surprise that Constantine did not return to his captor! Instead, after his father died, he demanded that he be recognized as the co-emperor in his father's place. Galerius never did fight Constantine, because he became ill and died soon afterward.

Narration Break: Talk about why some Jews don't believe that Jesus is the Messiah, while others accept Him (these are called Messianic Jews). Why do you think Diocletian's plan of splitting the empire did not work?

By AD 312, the co-emperors, Constantine and the new emperor of the Eastern Empire, Maxentius (max-ENN-she-us), were fighting each other for power over the entire empire. As Constantine approached Rome, with intentions to attack Maxentius the next day, an event occurred and changed history forever.

We don't know exactly what happened that night, but most historians give this account: As Constantine was sleeping during the night before his attack on Rome, he claimed to have seen the cross of the Christian God. He took this as a sign that this God was on his side. He instructed his men to paint white, Christian crosses on their shields. Constantine did win the battle against Maxentius that day and became known as the first Christian Roman Emperor. Whether or not he was actually a Christian is questionable. Some Christian historians believe that Constantine worshipped Jesus as the Roman Sun-god; this confusion is understandable because after all, Christ is the Son of God!

News of Constantine's conversion reached far and wide. The Christians came out of hiding and rejoiced because their emperor was on their side for the first time in history. Constantine granted the church overseers - now commonly called priests - favors, because he viewed Jesus as his "patron saint." These are the words

Constantine and his co-emperor, Licinius, issued in the Edict of Milan: "Our purpose is to allow Christians and all others to worship as they desire, so that whatever Divinity lives in the heavens will be kind to us."

Shortly after this, a group from the North African church asked Constantine to decide who could ordain an overseer (priest). This may seem trivial, but it was actually a monumental event. Because of this decision, the government and the church would be joined for the next twelve hundred years, and the government would "sponsor" the beliefs of the Church. The Church no longer lived as a sub-culture; they now enjoyed an elevated status. From that time on, the Church would be a major influential force throughout the world.

In the year 320, Licinius, the emperor of the Eastern Empire, went back on his word, which he had agreed upon when he and Constantine had drafted the Edict of Milan, and started persecuting the Christians. Of course this challenged Constantine to fight him, and soon the two were at war. After several years of war between the two empires, Constantine defeated Licinius and his army. Shortly after this, Constantine sentenced Licinius to death, along with Licinius' son. Constantine was now ruler of both the Western and Eastern Empire. The defeat of Licinius soon came to represent the downfall of the Greek-speaking, pagan, political power in the Eastern Empire. The predominately Christian, Latin-speaking Western Empire, which was centered around their capital city, Rome, decided that the Eastern Empire needed a new capital city to show that the Roman Empire was united and whole. They believed that this new capital city should be a center of impressive art and learning.

Chapter 2

Constantine chose the Greek city of Byzantium to become his new capital city, which he renamed Constantinople. A massive amount of work went into constructing this city; everything from marble statues, doors, and tiles were gathered from throughout the empire for use in this new city. After Constantine moved into his new capital city, he did his best to unite his kingdom. He dealt with any division in the Church as an (self-appointed) overseer and apostle. The years that followed were somewhat prosperous and peaceful for the Roman Empire.

It seemed that Diocletian's plan to unite the empire had finally worked. Constantine was mostly successful in his wars against the invading Barbarians, and the Church grew and flourished. The Roman Empire was united and strong again... Or was it?

Narration Break: Discuss Constantine. What do you think of this man?

Chapter 3

A Visit to the East

The Golden Age of India...

While the Roman Empire was struggling through their identity crisis in the West, the civilizations of the rest of the world were also moving into the Middle Ages. Because it is impossible to learn about everything that happens simultaneously, but in different places on earth, we have to do a little "continent-skipping."

In this chapter, we are going to shift our gaze from the Middle East to the Far East. Our first stop is the diamond-shaped country of India. India's natural, northern border is made up of the Indus River, running along its northwestern edge (the land surrounding this river is now the country of Pakistan), and the Himalayan Mountain range and Ganges River, along the northeastern edge. These natural barriers protected India from much of the Barbarian invasion that the rest of Europe and Asia were enduring throughout these centuries.

The land of India is vast, with a multitude of various terrains. The Himalayan Mountains and Ganges River in the north create a lush environment for an extensive variety of animals and plants. This habitat ends rather abruptly when you leave the Ganges River area and travel either south or west. This is the Thar desert, and as you would expect a desert to be, it is hot and sandy. Take a few moments to study the map of India.

In their ancient days, the people of this civilization first came to be farmers and merchants along the banks of the Indus River. They eventually became known as the Indus Valley Civilization and had quite an impact on the world of art, architecture, and pottery. During the ancient days, the people of India lived scattered here and there, mostly in the northern part of the peninsula. The mountains, rivers, and deserts made it easy to have separate kingdoms and tribes all living independently from each other, each with their own kings. Although the people of India were separated geographically, they were united by their religions, Hinduism and Buddhism, which focused mainly on living peacefully and following a strict moral code. We are not going to do an indepth study on these religions; it is most important to remember that the people from India needed to hear about Jesus, the same as everyone else. This is how life in India was for hundreds and hundreds of years.

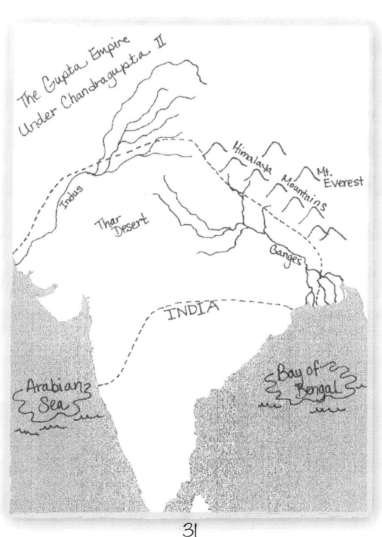

Around the year AD 319, a king of a small kingdom near the Ganges River decided that he would like to unite all of the kingdoms of the northern part of India. King Chandragupta (CHAWN-dru-GOOP-tuh) began to conquer little kingdoms near his. Chandragupta's son, Samudragupta (SAW-moo-dru-GOOP-tuh), and his grandson, Chandragupta II, both conquered more and more kingdoms, until they ruled all of northern India. We call this the Gupta Empire or the Gupta Dynasty.

Under the Gupta Dynasty, which lasted from AD 320 to 550, India flourished and prospered. Art, poetry, and literature made significant advances. Sculptors created amazing works of art from iron and copper, and scholars wrote books about mathematics and astronomy. Medical advances were also plentiful during the Gupta Dynasty. India had become united, peaceful, and rich. They felt safe, with their strong, well-trained army.

Do you remember how we learned about the Barbarian tribes that swept in from the north to attack the Roman Empire? During the AD 400s, a Barbarian tribe, called the Huns, flooded over the northern border of India and attacked the Gupta Empire. King Skandagupta (SKAWN-du-GOOP-tuh) united the armies of India to stop the Barbarian attack. When they were able to withstand the Huns, the people of India gave their king the credit for unifying their forces against the Barbarians. King Skandagupta was heralded as "favored by the gods" and honored by having his face stamped on the coins of the kingdom.

The wars with the Huns had weakened the Gupta Empire, however, and little by little, small sections of the kingdom broke away and became independent again. By the year AD 550, the Gupta Dynasty had come to an end, and the Golden Age of India had come to a close. The next dynasty would be established by a man named Harsha, from a branch of "White Huns," who had migrated into India, taken on many of the Indian customs, and woven themselves into fabric of the Indian culture.

Narration Break: <u>Talk about the early centuries of India's history. Study a map of India and discuss how it is protected from the rest of the content.</u>

The Imperial House of Japan...

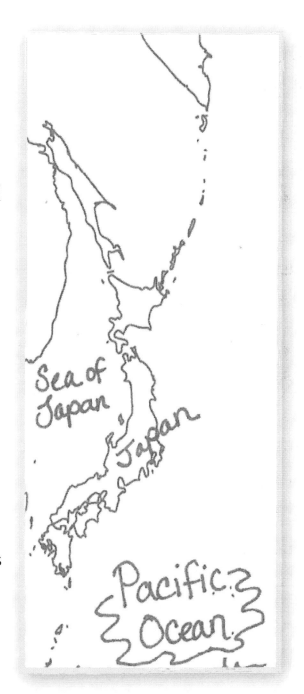

As we continue on our journey, we will travel east out of India, through Asia, until we come to the Sea of Japan. From there it's a trip across the water to the Japanese archipelago. Do you know what an archipelago is? Study the map of Japan and see if you can guess.

If you guessed that an archipelago is a stretch of water with a long line of islands, then you guessed right. In this case, the islands make up the country of

Japan. The four large islands, which make up the main part of the country, are surrounded by thousands of smaller islands. The Japanese Archipelago is so long, that its northern end is in subarctic zones, while the southern end is subtropical. As you can imagine, the plant and animal kingdoms are also extremely diverse because of this wide range in temperatures.

Like India, Ancient Japan was divided into many smaller tribes or clans, and also like India, a strong ruler arose from one of these smaller kingdoms to gain the rule of the entire country. The Yamato Clan became stronger and stronger, and within about two hundred years, they had conquered the surrounding clans and had become the rulers of all of Japan. Interestingly enough, this dynasty is still on the Japanese throne even now!

The people of Japan worshipped many gods and were given to many superstitions. One of the ways the Yamato Clan came to power is by saying that they were descendants of these gods. They also told tales of how they had conquered evil gods to gain the favor of the good gods. Perhaps more than any other reason, they gained favor with their countrymen, because they were excellent fighters. Becoming the rulers of all of Japan was a difficult accomplishment, but staying the rulers was even harder! The Yamato emperors borrowed ideas and methods of ruling from their neighbors across the Sea of Japan. China, the giant of the Orient, and a small, but powerful country situated between Japan and China, Korea. These two countries had a powerful influence on Japan's culture.

The Three Kingdom Period of Korea...

As is true with all of the countries of the world, Korea's history is long and complex. There is no way for us to delve deeply into any particular period of any given nation, so we will choose the highlights of a certain time period to discuss.

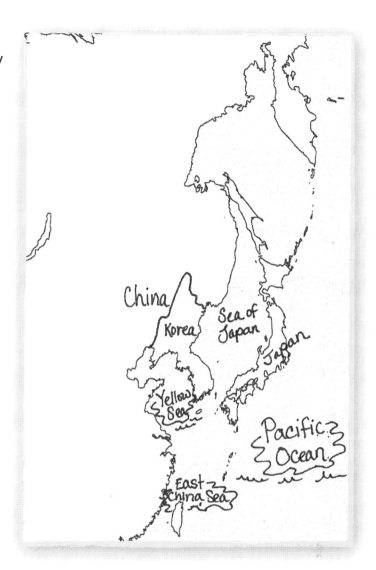

The Three Kingdom Period of Korea refers to the years between about AD 57 through 668. It is called the Three Kingdom Period, because there were three major kingdoms in Korea at that time. Before this time, Korea had been ruled by China, but the Koreans had rebelled and fought for their freedom. Even though they had won their independence, the Korean culture had been heavily influenced by the Chinese. Most Koreans spoke and wrote in Chinese. Their religion had also been influenced by China and many people observed the ways of Buddha.

Baekje (BIKE-shay), the kingdom closest to the Sea of Japan, decided that they wanted to try to get Japan to be their friend. They had ulterior motives, though; they wanted help conquering the other two kingdoms of Korea. They sent presents to the Yamato emperor to try to impress him.

The Japanese emperor was impressed with the gifts, especially a book written in Chinese. They wanted to know how to read this foreign language, and so they requested that a tutor be sent to Japan.

The Korean teacher taught the Emperor and his family how to read and write in Chinese and also about the ways of Buddha. Before long, many Japanese people were reading and writing in Chinese and following the ways of Buddha. Chinese had become the language of the higher class Japanese; only the common folk spoke Japanese. In this way, Korea and Japan were very much like China!   They enjoyed the Chinese culture and ways of doing things so much that it was almost as though China had invaded and set up their rule. However, China still wanted to rule Korea and Japan completely.

China attacked Korea and wiped out the Baekje Kingdom, and Japan, knowing they were probably next, sent in troops to help. Japan didn't want to be Chinese, so after they helped the Korean kingdoms push the Chinese back, they became completely independent from China. They no longer talked Chinese, dressed Chinese, or used Chinese goods. They worked hard to become uniquely Japanese again. This was difficult, because they had been doing everything the Chinese way for hundreds of years!

Japan is called the "Land of the Rising Sun," while China is called the "Land of the Setting Sun." Why do you think they are called this? Japan is to the east, where the sun rises, and China is to the west, where it sets. Both Japan and China thought of themselves as great nations, and both wanted to be the land of the sun.

Narration Break: Talk about the relationship between China, Japan, and Korea.

Chapter 4

A Look at the Maya & a Bible Called the Vulgate

The Great Maya Civilization...

In our last chapter, we visited a few of the countries making up the massive continent of Asia. If we continued east from Japan, we would be traveling over the great Pacific Ocean, toward the continents of North and South America and the stretch of land connecting these two giants. This connecting piece of land, Central America, technically belongs to North America and is the focus of the first part of this chapter. This area is also called Mesoamerica (MESS-o-a-MER-i-ca), which represents a mix of cultural characteristics, all developed and shared by a number of civilizations in the Central American area.

If you were with me in Volume 4, you may remember how we learned about some of the interesting, ancient tribes of the Americas. We discovered the Olmecs, who left behind some extremely intriguing artifacts and ruins of ancient temples and pyramids in Central America. We also learned about the fascinating, gigantic ground drawings, which the Nasca Indians left etched in the earth, and the magnificent, deserted city of Machu Picchu, which the Incan Indians left high in the Andes Mountains.

It is not clearly understood when the Maya civilization began, but many historians believe that the first of their settlements was established in 1800 BC. The Maya's territory covered what is now Guatemala, Belize, the western part of Honduras, and the very northern part of El Salvador. Most of this civilization was located on the Yucatán Peninsula, which separates the Gulf of Mexico and the Caribbean Sea.

Many of the Mayan's "books" and records were destroyed many hundreds of years later, at the time of the Spanish invasions. The artifacts and ruins left behind, give us a glimpse into the lives of these people. Their artwork and pottery have been found in many locations hundreds of miles from their homeland. Written inscriptions, in Mayan hieroglyphics, date back to the year 250 BC and give us a look at their written language, and their rather lavish culture.

Science and astronomy were very important to the Maya because they were closely linked to their religious practices. As they studied the moon, stars, and planets, they developed a complicated calendar for counting the days and years. (This calendar has caused many "end of the world" predictions throughout the centuries since the time of the Maya.) They kept impeccable records of what they studied in the heavens, charting the paths of celestial bodies and recording events such as eclipses, solstices, and equinoxes.

Why did the Maya create such elaborate calendars predicting when catastrophic happenings would occur? Just like everyone else at that time, the Maya did not have access to charts of the stars or written documentation of when solar eclipses would take place. In fact, they did not even understand what an eclipse was. (Remember, at this time, there were no high-powered telescopes with which to study the universe.) All they had were the records they kept of the obvious paths of certain bright "stars" or other heavenly bodies. They even speculated about certain heavenly features that were not discovered until much later.

These records show that the Maya were surprisingly accurate in their predictions, but of course, they did not know when the end of the earth would happen. The Bible tells us that no one but God knows this information. At the time of the Maya, people thought the earth was the center of the universe. (We will learn more about this later.) There are no records showing that the Maya believed any differently about the position of the earth in relationship to the sun.

Some people consider the Maya to be brilliant scientists, but in reality, they believed the heavens were held up by four jaguars, one at each corner. Even though they were excellent record-keepers, the Maya believed in mythology, which, in many ways, kept them from really understanding what they were seeing when they studied the heavens. They worshipped the rain, earth, plant and animal gods. Because of this, when they studied the heavens, they believed they were actually watching distant gods that might intend to either "bless" them or "curse" them.

The Maya civilization was organized into city-states, and the population numbered in the millions. Their palaces, cities, and monuments were elaborate in design. Perhaps the most famous of all of the Maya monuments is the stepped pyramids, which they built in their religious centers. These pyramids stand over one hundred feet tall, and in many cases, were built near the palaces of the rulers. Information about the rulers' genealogy and military accomplishments were inscribed, in hieroglyphics, on rock slabs and placed near the palaces and pyramids. All of these amazing architectural feats were accomplished without the help of metal tools or even the wheel!

The great Maya civilization would thrive for hundreds of years before declining. There are many theories why the civilization finally collapsed, but we do know that the complete and final ruin came when the Spanish conquistadors came across the Atlantic Ocean to conquer the Yucatán Peninsula in the 1500s. (We will study this event in our next volume of history.)

Narration Break: Talk about the Maya civilization. Talk about their "science" of studying the stars. How do you think believing in mythology would keep them from understanding the heavens?

Meanwhile, back in the Middle East...

For the rest of this chapter, we are going to return to the "center of civilization," as the Roman Empire believed itself to be. Sometimes the events of history line up in such a way that it is impossible to tell what happened first and started a chain of events. Many times, we are forced to look at something from many different angles to acquire a more complete understanding.

Do you remember the Roman Emperor we learned about in Chapter 2? His name was Constantine, and he was the son of one of the four rulers of Rome, set up by Emperor Diocletian. Remember, Diocletian was the emperor who thought dividing the Roman Empire into two parts would make it easier to rule and protect. As we learned in Chapter 2, this did not work too well, but when Constantine became the emperor, he did what he could to reunite the empire. The Roman Empire remained divided into two distinct sections, but under Constantine, it was more united than it was before.

Constantine also became very friendly with the Church. At this time in history, there were no separate, official denominations. The Christian Church was just that, although, I am sure there were groups of Christians who preferred to worship certain ways and held certain beliefs. Emperor Constantine became the first Roman emperor who actually got involved with the Church's decision-making, though, and this set a precedence that would be followed for a very long time.

Although the early Church is not the focus of this history volume, I do believe it is necessary to show how the Church was so closely and intricately intertwined with the Roman culture of this time. It would be impossible to understand the flow of history if one or the other was left out of the story. I understand that there are many types of families reading this story together, and I will do my best not to portray the Christian Church history from any particular angle or bias.

At this time in history, the Christian Church, as it was called at this point in time, was relatively new. Christ had come, as a baby, died, risen, and ascended into heaven two to three hundred years before this time. His followers had written down their accounts of His healing, walking on water, loving the unlovable, and making the final sacrifice on the cross. The Church was surprisingly still united on most of the

important issues; however, little by little, the leaders, who were in charge of the Church had, in some ways, overstepped their authority. In trying to protect the original teachings and writings of the Apostolic Elders, they went through great pains to trace their teachings back to the apostles. There was nothing wrong with that, but when they started tracing their *authority* back to the apostles as well, their roles in the Church started to shift ever so slightly.

These leaders, also called overseers or popes (which is the Latin word for "father"), took care of God's people throughout entire regions. Please remember, at this time in history, Christians were persecuted by many who did not understand them, so it was important to have strong leaders who knew how to care for the flock. Men and women, who wanted to dedicate themselves to God's work and not live by the standards of the world, lived in and worked from monasteries and convents. Many wonderful Christians served the needy and destitute in their communities.

One of these overseers, Polycarp, was a Greek Church leader in Asia Minor. Polycarp, who was eventually martyred for his faith, taught every believer to be the protector of the apostles' teachings. However, as the overseers gained more and more authority, "A priesthood of church leaders was beginning to supplant the priesthood of all believers."[1]

When Constantine came on the scene, the Church had well established boundaries, with overseers working to care for those in their areas. Constantine made himself an overseer and therefore became a leader of the Church. As a leader of the Church, Constantine found himself in the middle of a disagreement between an overseer from Alexandria, Egypt, and almost the entire remainder of the Church.

This overseer, Arius, taught that Jesus was not really eternal God. Instead, he taught that Jesus was the first being that God created. Of course, this angered many of the other overseers, and in 325 AD, a council was called in Nicaea, a small town in northern Asia Minor. Overseers, from all over the world, came to the council to discuss the disturbances caused by Arius' teachings. Constantine was there and called the assembly together.

After many angry outbursts and arguments about what to do with this wayward overseer, it was decided that a creed should be written to outline in clear wording, what the foundational beliefs of the Church were exactly. This creed would exclude the heresy being taught by Arius and would set the grounds to excommunicate him from the church. The document that came from this decision is called the "Creed of Nicaea." Much to Constantine's relief, this council seemed to bring peace back to the church and to the empire as well.

It was also around this time that the need for a Bible, written in the language of the common person, became more and more in demand. Up until this point, the Scriptures were either in the original, ancient languages of Hebrew, Greek, or Aramaic. Most people of the Middle Ages did not speak these languages; if they could read or write at all, it was in Latin.

In AD 405, a monk, named Jerome, set to work to translate the Bible into Latin. It took him twenty-two years to complete this monumental project. When he was finished, some people didn't like Jerome's translation because he didn't translate from the old Greek text of the Jewish manuscripts. Instead, he translated directly from the original Hebrew. Also, his translation used words which were more easily understood by the average person of the day. Some people thought his translation was "Vulgate," which is Latin for "Common" or "Vulgar." (To this day, this version of the Bible is still called the Vulgate.) Of course, when people realized that they could easily read this new translation, they liked it!

Narration Break: How did the Early Church affect the Roman Culture? Talk about the Vulgate.

Chapter 5

Crash! There Goes the Western Roman Empire!

In this chapter, we will witness the complete collapse of the Western Roman Empire and how it affected the land it had once controlled. If you remember, we discovered that this part of the empire was the area surrounding the city of Rome in Italy. Rome had been the capital of the Roman Empire until Emperor Constantine made the city of Constantinople the new capital city in the year 330. After this move, the Western Empire became weaker and more susceptible to Barbarian attacks.

In 410, the city of Rome fell when the Barbarian leader, Alaric and his Goths, burned the ancient city and carried away the treasures. There was nothing left of the glory that was Rome. The Barbarian invasion, which had started centuries before, had finally brought an end to the empire. Do you remember how huge the Roman Empire had been at its pinnacle of world influence? It had wrapped its long fingers around territories all the way up into Europe, and now that the Roman Empire no longer existed, those lands were free of Roman control.

One of those northern lands was Britain, the home of the Celts, who had fought ferociously against the Roman invasion. The Celts were strong warriors and had kept the Romans from taking complete control of the their land, containing them, instead, to the southern part. When the Western Empire fell, the Celts gleefully drove out the remaining Roman soldiers, who were occupying Britain and took back complete control of Britain.

Celtic Warrior

These Celtic warriors were so proud of their fighting abilities, they made up stories to boast about it. These stories were made into songs called bards, which were sung almost like a news report, by traveling singers called minstrels. Of course, their stories became more and more akin to tall tales, but they were still appreciated by the patrons and owners of the inns and pubs, where they entertained the masses.

After the Barbarians had conquered Rome, they turned their attention elsewhere, including Britain. The Celts were not a united people, ruled by one king. Instead, they were similar to the people of India or Japan, before a strong king arose to unite the country. Actual happenings of this time period are rather sketchy, and many accounts that we do have actually come from the bards, passed down from one generation to the next for hundreds

Chapter 5

of years.

Some of these stories tell us that there was a Celtic king, who was stronger than all of the other kings in Britain. This king ruled a tribe in central Britain, and he became tired of fighting with the other Celtic clans surrounding him. (This is what the Celts did when they had no outside invaders - they fought each other to see who was the toughest and meanest.) Legend says that this strong Celtic King, Vortigern, wanted help, so he sent a message to two clans of Barbarians living to the north of him, across the North Sea. In his message, King Vortigern asked the leaders of the Barbarian clans to come help him fight the other Celts, and in return, he would allow them to live in Britain.

These Barbarian tribes, the Angles and the Saxons, decided to take the Celtic King up on his offer. After they had helped King Vortigern fight his enemies, they settled in the central part of Britain and invited more of their friends to come join them. Soon, the Celts were being run out of their own country, but by this time, there was nothing they could do about it; the Angles and the Saxons had taken over the southern and eastern part of Britain.

After the Anglo-Saxons - as they came to be called - had taken over a large part of Britain, they divided the land into seven kingdoms and set up rulers for each section. Today, we call this area England, which comes from the word, Angle or Angle-land. What do you think the Celts did with all of these Anglo-Saxons overrunning their land? Well, some of them decided to make the best of it and learn to live with these new people, while others decided that because they just couldn't adjust, they would move. The group of Celts, who decided to leave, went west and north of England to live by themselves. Today, these lands are called Scotland, Ireland, and Wales.

The Seven Anglo-Saxon Kingdoms

As we have learned, the Celts made up songs to tell their tales of glory. They mostly did this because they did not have a well-established written language; therefore, they did not write anything down. When the Anglo-Saxons came to occupy Britain, they did not write their histories down either. This is the reason, we call this time period in Britain's history, the "Dark Years;" it's "dark" because we do not know what happened during that time period. Like the Celts, the Anglo-Saxons also passed their stories along by word of mouth. You may have heard one of these tales because it is still told today. "The Legend of Beowulf" has been passed down for hundreds of years. This legend is the one of the oldest pieces of literature in the English language.

Chapter 5

Have you ever played the game "Telephone"? If you have, you know how it goes, but for those of you who may not have played it, I will explain the process. First, ten or more players sit in a circle. Next, one player is chosen to be "it." This person has to think of something to say and then whisper it into their neighbor's ear. That person, in turn, whispers what they heard into the next player's ear, and so it goes, player by player, until everyone has heard. The last player, who is sitting next to the player who started the game, repeats out loud what they heard. It is amazing, and often times, hilarious, to hear what the original message has become, as it moves from person to person!

This is exactly what has happened with some of these legends. Even though the legend of Beowulf was recorded in writing, we are not sure how long it was told as a bard or poem. If you are interested in reading or hearing this story, there are written copies and audio versions available, as well as some in more simplified, reader-friendly form.

Narration Break: Talk about the Celts and how the Anglo-Saxons came to be in Britain. Find England on a map and discover where this part of our story takes place.

Do you remember what the church leaders were called at this time in history? That's right, they were called overseers or popes. As we discussed in our earlier chapters, church history and world history had become intertwined during the reign of Emperor Constantine. By this time in history (the mid to late 400s), the church had gained a powerful position in politics, but what happened after the fall of Rome? You might think the church would also fall, but Christianity is not based on who is in power, or who is the ruler on earth.

Chapter 5

The Roman citizens were frightened! They did not know who was in charge, because even though the Barbarians were fierce fighters, they were not good at ruling. As they went around fighting and conquering, they often did not set up governments to rule the land which they had just rampaged. Many Roman citizens turned to the church for help. They knew they could at least receive help from the monks and nuns who served the community.

One of these overseers became instrumental in taking the gospel to the land of the Angle-Saxons. The Celts had heard about Christ a long time before this, but when the Angles and the Saxons had flooded their land, their churches had been destroyed. In their place, the Angles and Saxons had set up idols and images of their own gods, which were many! This is the story of Gregory, the overseer who wanted to evangelize the Anglo-Saxons.

Gregory had started as a monk, but he was promoted to overseer of Rome when his predecessor died of the plague. One story says that Gregory was walking in the marketplace and witnessed a slave auction. As he approached, he saw men, women, and even children being sold as slaves. Gregory walked closer, and his attention was drawn to a group of young boys. These boys had very pale skin tones and blond hair. Gregory had never seen such light complected children, so he asked the children from what land they were brought.

The boys answered Gregory, that they were Anglo-Saxons from Britain, which was ruled by King Aella. Gregory thought this sounded like "Alleluia," and he took this as a sign that he needed to tell the Britons about God. He decided that he would send a group of monks to minister with missionary work to the Anglo-Saxons.

Chapter 5

Around the year 497, a group of forty-one monks arrived in Britain. To be honest, some of these monks were not excited about being missionaries to these "Barbarians," but they served anyway. The good news of the gospel spread quickly into the darkness, and by Christmas, just a few years later, thousands of Anglo-Saxons had become Christians. One of these missionary monks was named Augustine.

History calls this monk Augustine of Canterbury because the monks, who went to Britain to evangelize the Anglo-Saxons, settled in a coastal village named Canterbury. (I don't think any of the monks sent on this mission were expecting to have so much success.) As Christianity spread throughout Britain, many Anglo-Saxon and Irishmen decided to become monks. These monks built great, beautiful monasteries in which to live.

These monks worked hard to help spread the good news of the Gospel and to help those in need around them. Life in a monastery was a bit different than your life, I am sure! At this time in church history (and still in some places today), people of the church thought that denying themselves physical comfort or pleasure would cause them to be closer to God. Because of this closely held belief, the monks who lived in monasteries, and the nuns who lived in convents, led extremely simple lives. They had the very barest of necessities in life, worked long, hard hours, and never married or had children.

The monks had another important job: they wrote copies of the Bible and other Christian literature. Why would they do this? Well, during the Middle Ages, there were no printing presses yet, and there were no bookstores like we have today. As I am writing this book, I am sitting in my office chair, typing away on a computer. If I make a mistake, I can easily hit the backspace key, and Viola!, the mistake is gone. I don't have to dip a pen into a bottle of ink and write slowly and carefully on parchment paper - and thank goodness, too! It would take me a very long time indeed to complete a book! The monks did not even have paper or parchment unless they made it. They truly made each book "from scratch."

First, they made parchment by soaking, stretching, scraping, and drying animal skins. Next, they made ink by soaking, mashing, and straining certain berries and fruits. Then, they made pens by chiseling and sharpening goose quills. The books they created were not just words written carefully on a page; they were masterpieces! There are still many samples of these monks' handwritten books available to see today, and if you ever get the chance to view them, I am sure you will be amazed at the artwork decorating the pages.

These books also record messages that the monks wrote to each other. The monks working in the scriptorium (the writing room) were supposed to be silent, as to not interrupt the writing progress, but many of them wrote little notes to each other on the corners of the book pages! You can still see these notes on the pages of these well-preserved books.

It is important to remember, during this hard time in history, when the largest empire in the world had shaken and fallen to Barbarians, many people turned to the church for help and stability. In our next chapter, we will discover what happened to the Eastern Roman Empire during this time.

Narration Break:

How did the fall of the Western Roman Empire affect the world? How did the church help?

Chapter 6

Byzantine Rulers, King Arthur, and Knights

Justinian and Theodora...

Several chapters ago, we learned that the capital city of the Roman Empire was moved from Rome, in the Western Empire, to Constantinople in the Eastern Empire. Barbarians had nibbled away at the Western Empire until it finally fell, but what about the Eastern Empire?

The Eastern Empire had also been subject to the attacks, but they had managed to ward off the Barbarians. Even though they lost a large portion of land to the Barbarians, and their empire shrank to the area directly surrounding Constantinople, the Eastern Empire survived.

We call this surviving part of the Roman Empire, the Byzantine (BIZ-in-teen) Empire. The Byzantine Empire may have started out small, but it certainly did not stay that way. Eventually, strong emperors came to the Byzantine throne. These emperors fought and conquered sections of the surrounding area, until soon, the Byzantine Empire was spreading out all the way around the Mediterranean Sea.

One of the most powerful Byzantine emperors was Justinian. Emperor Justinian was not born into a royal family; in fact, he was not even from a rich, influential family. Justinian grew up as a poor, country boy. His parents were farmers, and they worked hard to feed their family. Justinian's mother had a brother named Justin, who was a high-ranking officer in the imperial guard. Uncle Justin knew that his nephew did not have much of a chance to make something of himself if he did not go to school. So it was that Justinian's uncle took him to Constantinople, where there were many renowned institutions of education.

After he finished school, Justinian decided to go into the army. Everyone liked this bright, organized, young man. He was helpful to his officers, and he gained respect for his bravery. As you might expect from such a young man, he moved quickly up through the ranks in the army. Many people thought he would make a wonderful emperor, and when his uncle, who had become the emperor, died, that is exactly what happened!

Emperor Justinian was a great leader. He did not like the fact that his empire was so small, so he decided to do something about it. After building up his army, he set out to conquer the lands that used to belong to the Eastern Roman Empire. Soon, the Byzantine Empire was the leading power in the world.

Emperor Justinian did not rule his empire alone; he had a wise and helpful wife.

Chapter 6

This is how they met...

It just so happened, that there was a lovely, young woman named Theodora, who lived in Constantinople. Theodora had grown up in a family, who owned a circus. From a very young age, Theodora worked with the animals in the circus. She led a wild and ungodly life, but when she grew up, Theodora became a Christian and gave up her life in the circus. She decided to move to Constantinople to live a quiet, useful life.

One day, Justinian, who was, at this time, a soldier in the army, rode through the streets of Constantinople. He saw Theodora standing by the side of the road. He was enthralled by her beauty and asked about her. No one knew who she was, so Justinian searched and searched until he found out where her home was. When he had finally found her, Justinian asked her to marry him. When Justinian became emperor, Theodora became the empress of the Byzantine Empire. Empress Theodora is thought by many to be the most powerful woman in both the history of the Roman Empire and Byzantine Empire.

There was so much wealth in the Byzantine culture that the glory, that was Rome, paled in comparison. The Byzantine children attended school to learn from the philosophers of the day. They were taught by strict professors, who oversaw the educational process with watchful eyes. The architectural glory in the city of Constantinople was astounding! There were beautiful palaces, schools, and churches in abundance. Homes were emblazoned with mosaics made of precious stones, gold, and colorful glass.

Chapter 6

The most famous and beautiful church in Constantinople was called the Hagia Sophia (HAZSH-ee-uh so-FEE-uh). This church was really a great cathedral, with huge, open spaces, beautiful windows, intricate mosaics, and huge domes. Indeed, it is considered an architectural wonder of the world. (The Hagia Sophia is now a museum, but has spent its life being a cathedral and a Muslim mosque, but we will learn about that later.)

The Christian church in the East was different than the church in the West. We learned that the church in the West was mostly run by the Pope; the church in the East did not agree with this. They believed that all believers should have a voice in the church. They considered themselves brothers in Christ with their fellow believers in the West, but they did not consider themselves part of the same type of church. There was much division creeping into the Christian church.

Narration Break: Retell the story of Justinian and Theodora. How was the Byzantine Empire different than the Roman Empire? How was it similar? Find some pictures of the Hagia Sophia.

Sometimes in history, a character, who is so hidden in shadow of legend and mystery, comes along, and we wonder who they truly are. Some historians argue that there is not enough historical evidence to prove this man even existed, but there are enough Medieval records to the contrary to make me want to include his name in our story.

The story of King Arthur was first discovered in the Annales Cambriae (The Annals of Wales), the Historia Brittonum (the rather legendary, purported history of the British), and the writings of a prominent church figure named Gildas. Despite the appearance of the story of Arthur in all three of these literary sources, modern historians doubt Arthur is real. Remember that the

Anglo-Saxons were trying to take over Britain during this time. Also during this time period, events were sung about, not written down.

According to the bards and folklore, King Arthur was a British leader in the late 400s and early 500s. His many exploits as a leader are recorded in legends and Medieval romances. I think most of us have heard at least one version of the story of King Arthur, who had a legendary round table, knights, and a queen named Guinevere. It is believed that King Arthur was a British battle-chief, who won twelve battles against invading Barbarians from the North, when they broke through Hadrian's Wall. Hadrian's Wall was built starting in AD 122, by the Roman emperor, Hadrian. The wall served as a protection for the citizens of Southern Britain. If you would like to read the legend of King Arthur, there are plenty of versions available!

The Making of a Knight...

Let's take a look at another interesting topic, the Medieval knight. Have you ever seen a suit of armor? If you have, you know that it is all metal. How did these men, not only walk around in armor, but also fight and ride horses in it? There were various types of armor, but the average suit weighed anywhere between forty-five and seventy-five pounds! Even the horse wore armor to protect it during battle. Clank! Clank!

So, what did it take to become a knight? Do you think you would want to be one? Besides being strong enough to wear all of that heavy armor, knights had to be brave, willing to fight, and even willing to die. They went through a long training and testing period, and they had to follow a certain code - the Code of Chivalry. The word "chivalry" and the idea for the code, came from a group of lords in France during the twelfth century. The French word for horse is "cheval." These French lords followed a strict code of conduct, and soon all knights were expected to follow it also.

The Code of Chivalry was not an easy code to follow. First, the chivalrous knight had to be extremely brave. In fact, he had to be willing to do anything he was asked to do, even if it seemed foolhardy. Second, the chivalrous knight had to be honorable. This means that, he not only had to be brave, he had to be polite and fair while he was doing his brave deeds. It was this honorable behavior that set knights apart from other types of warriors of the day. While other warriors were sometimes rather rude in their behavior, knights were expected to be polite and chivalrous at all times.

Of course, the knights did not just decide to become a knight, and that was that. No, indeed! They not only had to go through rigorous training, many times they had to work their way up to that privilege. A boy who wanted to be a knight had to start out as a page for another knight or even to a group of knights working for a lord of a manor. His job would be to clean up after the knights, including washing their laundry and shining their armor. When the page had grown a little, he might be made a squire. At this level, he was given the job of caring for his lord's horses, or cleaning and polishing the lord's armor. He might be chosen to help the lord get his armor on. It was around this time that the "knight-want-to-be" would be introduced to weaponry. He would start trying to build muscles so he could lift the heavy swords, wear armor, and learn the art of fencing.

Knights ALWAYS took care of those smaller than themselves, were polite even when they were fighting, and always took care of their captured enemies.

Knights NEVER attacked from behind or ran away and left a friend in need.

So, how is your family?

They are well. Thanks for asking!

Chapter 6

Next, the knight-in-training would be allowed to ride the horses and learn to fight from there. This training included learning how to joust. The knight-in-training would be learning the Code of Chivalry during this time. By the time the young knight was twenty years old, he was expected to have learned everything he needed to know.

Narration Break:

Do you know the story of King Arthur? What did it take to become a knight?

Chapter 7

Daily Life in the Middle Ages

In this chapter we are going to take a sweeping look at life in the Middle Ages, from the fall of the Western Roman Empire through the end of the time period we are studying in this book. I feel that it is important to have a backdrop in our minds on which we can pin important events that we will learn about throughout the rest of our study. First, we will discuss the repercussions of the fall of the Western Roman Empire. We will also look at the rather make-shift government and social system that arose from the ashes of its destruction. Later in the chapter, we will take a look at the culture, homes, and kingdoms, which were common in this time period.

The Feudal System...

When the dust settled after the collapse of the Western Roman Empire, panic began to set in. There was no longer a central government, therefore, there were no schools or law enforcement officers. No one knew who would lead them, teach them, or protect them. There was no longer a monetary system, and the old Roman coins were worth nothing more than the metal they were made of. Suddenly, even people who had been rich became paupers overnight.

It soon became apparent that those who owned large amounts of land were the new "top dogs." These large-land barons became powerful men very quickly, because their land produced food on which everyone depended. It seemed the rest of the population was at the mercy of these new barons.

Many times, these newly-powerful barons funded the churches if the overseers did what they were told. A new cultural and government system was starting to emerge: the Feudal System. This new way of life was truly based on the principle of "the strongest survive." The richest were at the top of the status ladder, with everyone else jostling for position under them.

The poor people, who did not own land, worked for the barons. These people were called serfs, and their wages were: enough food to keep them alive, a ramshackle cottage or hut to live in with their families, and a job. There was not much hope of improving their position. This was a time of desperation for many common-folk, as they eked out a living from the hard ground of the masters' fields. Every family member was expected to work long, hard hours; they were more slave than servant. While the serfs lived in shacks, the land barons lived in manors - huge houses or castles.

Some of these landowners became so powerful, they were given the titles that royal families use, such as "Lord," "Sir," "Lady," "Baron," or "Your Lordship." Soon, the land barons were building up their own little kingdoms. The profits from the barons' lands were huge, and trading with surrounding landowners made them even wealthier. The huge landowners built up their holdings by conquering the smaller landowners around them.

Some of these barons conquered enough, they became the king of their own kingdoms. These kings ruled over the barons, even though they were almost equal in power. The barons had their own armies of knights to protect their lands and to fight with the other Lords around them. Sometimes the baron would divide the land out amongst their loyal knights and make them his officers. These knights would sometimes work hard to move up in rank, and if the Lord of the manor did not have a son, the knight might be named to inherit the Lord's holdings. Study the drawing on the next page. Can you see how the feudal system is arranged? How would you like to be stuck at the bottom of such an arrangement?

As you can see, the king is at the top, peasants are at the bottom, and the knights are in the middle. As we learned in our last chapter, if a knight could work hard enough to be promoted to a higher position, he might receive a piece of land as a reward from his king. This land, along with its accompanying manor or castle, was called a fief (FEE). The fief was farmed by the peasants - farmer serfs - who produced enough to pay the taxes and support the knight and his family. In turn, the knight and his men fought to protect the baron.

When the king needed to make everyone support an idea or a project that he wanted to do, he called together all of the villagers and knights living in his kingdom. At this gathering, he would ask for their support. (This is believed to be the beginning of the parliament systems of Europe.)

All across the land that used to be the Western Roman Empire, a new world culture emerged. There was no longer a huge, powerful empire ruling vast stretches of land. As centuries passed, these lands all across Europe organized into separate countries, as alliances were made between kingdoms, with kings, emperors, and barons. As you can imagine, the Feudal System was not a uniform system of government; it varied from place to place and from century to century.

Narration Break: Discuss the Feudal System. How and why did it start?

Castles...

Now let's take a look at castles. Have you ever wondered why the Medieval lords and kings built castles? (You may already know the answer to that question!) Castles became popular because they were more effective at keeping invaders out. They were big enough for the residing lord and lady to live comfortably with their family, and to also house the small army of knights who protected the family, along with the servants and caretakers of the estate.

Chapter 7

If you have ever seen a picture or a drawing of a castle, you know that these were very large structures. They were built out of brick and wood, and many times had a moat of water around them, which made them look like they were on a small island right in the middle of a pond. Whenever a castle had a moat surrounding its base, there was also a drawbridge. This bridge was kept drawn up against the side of the castle to keep out any unwanted visitors and lowered across the moat to allow welcomed guest to pass over into the castle.

As time went on, many barons and lords built huge castles for their families to live in. These castles had high walls, huge fireplaces, and towers, from which guards stood watch. You may think it would be fun to live in one of these castles, but unless you like to be cold and damp, a Medieval castle would not be a comfortable home. They did not have the electricity that makes modern day homes warm, so they were drafty and miserable, and there was no running water or indoor plumbing! How were these massive structures built? By the 1200s, the castles of Europe were quite fantastic!

Let's go through the steps of building a castle. Here is a fictional, though realistic, look at how a castle was built.

Somewhere in Britain or Wales, sometime in the thirteenth century...

In our story, the King of England has given a rich noble, Sir Charles, the job of being ruler of a certain area in Wales. Sir Charles has been living in Scotland with his family, but he decides that this is a good political move. After visiting Wales, he tells his wife, Lady Elizabeth, that he is going to take the job, but she doesn't have to pack yet; it will take at least four years to build the castle and at least four months to build their temporary home on their new estate in Wales. Lady Elizabeth sighs with relief.

Sir Charles sets out to find the perfect location for the town and castle that he intends to build. The location is important because it needs to be easy to fortify and protect. The castle will be in one corner of the town, connected by a wall and a series of towers and bridges. The town, which will consist mostly of homes for the peasants, who work the surrounding farmland and pay taxes to Sir Charles, will also be surrounded by a wall with watchtowers.

This is a huge project! Sir Charles will need hundreds of tradesmen to construct the town and castle. Word goes out around the countryside, advertising for masons, carpenters, quarrymen to dig and shape rocks, blacksmiths to keep tools in working order, mortar makers, and strong men to dig clay and rocks for the building project.

After the location for the town and castle are determined, the work begins at once. The first step in the building process is to make a temporary housing complex, barracks for the workers and knights that are there to guard the project and land, along with the temporary home for the royal family. Next, the diggers start digging a wide ditch all the way around the the circumference of the town and castle. This is where the wall will be built.

Sir Charles and the architects set to work on designing the castle, while work on the wall starts. The diggers find a deposit of good, solid limestone and the digging commences. Quarrymen direct the workers to which stones should be brought to the building site and soon, there are piles of stones and

rock ready to start the wall. Masons start situating the stones while mortar makers mix and carry large slabs of mortar to slather between the rocks.

It takes the men almost five years to finish the project, and by this time, the town has grown to several hundred occupants. Sir Charles, Lady Elizabeth, and the children move into the castle, and life settles into a routine.

An Age of Darkness...

Do you remember when I said that the church had become a powerful influence on the world? What was the name of the emperor who had joined the empire with the church? His name was Constantine. In a later chapter, we will learn about another king who would become an important character in church history, but in this chapter about castles and knights, I want to tell you a little more about how the church became more powerful.

As time progressed through the Middle Ages, the church took on another role in history. Priests were paid to serve the lords of the manors, and many did this willingly to keep their churches open. As we have learned throughout this chapter, these lords were often the only people who had any money, but it was also in this way, the rich became more and more powerful.

Remember, there were far fewer schools after the fall of the Roman Empire, and the daily focus of life was survival. For centuries, generation after generation of people worked hard to stay alive. Education became a rare gift for only the richest citizens. Fewer and fewer people could read. As the civilization slipped further and further into desperation and ignorance, the church relied more and more on fine buildings (funded by the lords of the manors), stained glass, and theatrical plays to try to teach the people about God. The preached and written word was being replaced by man-made architecture.

The majority of the population across Europe considered themselves to be Christian. The knights, whom we learned about in Chapter 6, considered themselves to be fighting not only for their manor's lord, but for the Lord God. They felt that they were earning a special place in heaven by fighting anyone who would come against their church or village.

Narration Break: Imagine living in a castle. What do you think your life would be like? How did the church's role change during this time in history?

Chapter 8

A Visit to China & a Firestorm Hits Europe

In Volume 4 of this history series, we learned that the land of China had not been a united country for many years. As in many other ancient civilizations, people had first settled along the rivers to farm and fish. Over the centuries, larger groups of people banded together to form clans scattered across the land. Finally, as is the case in almost all other growing civilizations, one, stronger leader arose above the others and conquered the rest of the clans around him.

As the centuries slowly rolled by, dynasty after dynasty took control of China, and eventually the nation was divided into two separate countries, the North and the South. This is how China remained for a very long time. There were hard feelings between the people of the North and the South; they each thought the other was barbaric and uncultured.

In the Northern army, there was a general who thought he could conquer the South and reunite the country. General Yang Jian (YANG she-IN) took his army and marched south to attack the king of the South. It was not a long war, for the North was strong and quickly conquered the South. Soon, General Yang Jian was the new emperor of all of China, and the beginning of a new dynasty, the Sui dynasty. What was he going to do with a badly fractured country full of a rather grumpy population?

General Yang Jian certainly had his work cut out for him. Besides having a difficult crowd to govern, Emperor Yang Jian had another problem, a more natural problem, which could be more of a threat to uniting the country of

China than the people themselves. There are two major rivers that flow east and west through the mainland of China. These rivers, the Yangtze River and the Yellow River, swell and become extremely wild during China's rainy season. It was nearly impossible for travelers to pass from North to South or from South to North. Without a way to travel north and south easily, how could they establish a common culture?

In the year 569, Yang Jian's son, Yangdi, who had become the next Sui emperor, decided to remedy the problem by making another river. This new river would be a man-made, hand-dug can that would connect the other two rivers, by flowing north and south between them. This man-made river would be called the Grand Canal, and it would take years and years to make.

To raise money for this huge project, the people of China were taxed heavily, and when this was not enough, they were commanded to pay their taxes for ten years in advance! Not only did the people have to endure these excessive tax laws, they were also commanded to work on the digging of the canal. Every man was commanded to spend time working on the canal, and every family had to send a woman, child, and elderly man also.

All of these taxes and laws, forcing the people of China to work on the canal, caused widespread poverty. Thousands of people died while working on the canal, for the work was hard, the conditions were wet and cold, and food was scarce. There were not enough people to farm the land and grow the crops for families because there were so many people working on the canal. Starvation was widespread, and poverty, caused by the high taxes, left thousands completely impoverished.

After the Grand Canal was finished, Emperor Yangdi demanded to be the first to ride down "his" man-made river. It took thousands of men to row the emperor's barges and boats, loaded with all kinds of riches, down the canal. There Emperor Yangdi was, floating grandly down the canal, which was dug by his countrymen and paid for by their money. Maybe it was during this grand ride down the canal that the emperor got the grand idea for other magnificent building projects his people could do for him.

In the years following the completion of the Grand Canal, Emperor Yangdi commanded that his subjects build him grand palaces, fancy arbor gardens, and many other grand-scale building projects. All of these were funded by the taxes cruelly imposed upon the people.

Finally, the people of China revolted and overthrew the crazy emperor, who had forced over eight million people to work as slaves for him. Yangdi's grandson tried to rule in his grandfather's place, but his rule was cut short when the people demanded for him to step down. So ended the Sui dynasty after only three emperors and forty years. The people of China were thankful to see them go as they welcomed the next emperor.

Emperor Li Yuang (LEE-you-ah) was the first emperor of the Tang dynasty. He was a much better ruler than those of the Sui dynasty. Emperor Li Yuang knew that if the people of China were unhappy, hungry, and impoverished, then he was not being a good ruler. When he came to the throne, China was not strong. Yangdi had stripped the people of their wealth and health in his quest to become the king with the most wealth. Emperor Li Yuang decided to rebuild the cities and towns of his country and to give his people more freedoms. He also encouraged his countrymen to trade with surrounding nations.

By creating a friendlier atmosphere in his country, Emperor Li Yuang helped China to rebuild. The Tang dynasty lasted over three hundred years, and once again, China became a strong and prosperous country. The years of the Tang dynasty are called the Golden Age of China. As the years passed, the people of China came out of their poverty and became rich and cultured. There were great pieces of art created during this time, and written pieces of literature were plentiful. Isn't it amazing how a ruler of a country can determine the demise or prosperity of the entire nation?

Narration Break: Discuss the Sui and Tang dynasties of China. How were they different from each other? Try to locate some pictures of the Grand Canal and pieces of art work from the Tang dynasty.

Chapter 8

If you were with me in Volume 4 of this series, you will remember that we learned about how one of Abraham's sons, Ishmael, became the "father" of a religion that is still on the earth today. Today, we are going to learn about how that religion, Islam, took root and quickly spread throughout the Middle East.

Our story starts in the seventh century AD, in the thick dust of the Arabian Peninsula, where tents of the wandering Beduins dotted the countryside. These Beduins were descendants of Ishmael, and they had roamed the desert for hundreds of years.

It was around the year 622, in the city of Mecca, that a simple Beduin man, name Muhammed, claimed to have been visited by the angel Gabriel. Muhammed did not like how many of his fellow Beduins lived; he was disturbed by their irresponsible behavior. As a young man, Muhammed had spent much time by himself praying to the Beduin gods.

Chapter 8

On this particular day, Muhammed had been praying in a cave, when he claimed to have received a vision about a god named Allah being the one true God. Muhammed ran home and told his family what he had been told; they believed him and called him a prophet. Soon, Muhammed was preaching to whomever would listen to him. His words encouraged his fellow countrymen to live more peacefully and to follow the commands he said had been given to him by Allah.

One of these commands said that people who had a lot of money should share it with those who did not have much. Of course, this was a popular idea with the poor people but not appreciated by the wealthy. Before long, there was even more division between the two classes, as the wealthy treated the lower class, who had converted to Islam, with contempt. As more and more people in Mecca converted to Islam, fewer and fewer of them went to the city to offer sacrifices to the other gods. This made the merchants who sold to the temple crowds, extremely angry.

Muhammed was forced to run away to a town called Medina. This journey from Mecca to Medina is called the Hegira. This event became the starting point on the Islamic calendar. Even today, the Muslims count the beginning date of their religion from that point. We count the years from Christ's advent here on Earth, so the current year at the time of the writing of this book, is 2013 - two thousand, thirteen years after Christ. The Muslims count from the date of the Hegira.

As Muhammed lived in Medina, he taught everyone about Allah and the teachings of his holy book, called the Koran. He became so popular, in fact, not just a prophet, but as a powerful ruler. Everyone thought he was extremely wise and came to him for advice. Muhammed decided that he wanted to rule Mecca also, so he started raiding camel trains traveling past Medina, taking supplies to Mecca. Soon armies from both cities were fighting each other. This went on for over seven years, before Mecca finally fell to Muhammed's ever-growing army of Muslims.

Muhammed became stronger and stronger, as tribe after tribe of Beduins converted to Islam. Soon, he ruled over the entire Arabian Peninsula, because he forced everyone to be Muslims or die. Islam was spreading, and even after Muhammed unexpectedly died, it continued to reach farther into Europe and Asia. After the death of Muhammed, one of his original followers became the new leader. These leaders were called caliphs, and they led their armies in wars against their neighbors.

The caliphs attacked the Byzantine empire and took away a large portion of their territory. They conquered and pillaged, and everywhere they went, they converted the citizens of their new territory to Islam. As the Islam empire moved north, they came to the banks of the great Tigris River, and there, they stopped and built a huge and majestic new capital city. This city was distinct because of its unique round shape. Bagdad became the home of the caliphs who ruled the Islamic empire.

We will learn more in a later chapter about the fight to keep Islam from spreading and taking over the world. For those of you who did not study through Volume 4, I am including a section from that story, which explains the roots of Islam. Even if you did complete Volume 4, I encourage you to read through the segment again. I believe that it is of extreme importance for all of us to understand where this religion was birthed, so that we can know more how to pray for those caught in the deception and darkness called Islam. Only when we understand Satan's schemes and lies, comparing them to the absolute truth of God Almighty's Word, can we stand strong in the truth.

From Volume 4 "The Story of the Ancients"

A son was born to Abraham from Hagar, but he was not the promised son. Sometimes we think that one little act of disobedience will not really hurt anyone, but as we are going to see in this chapter of our story, this is exceedingly untrue. This son, Ishmael, who was brought about through Hagar, would prove to be an act of disobedience which still troubles the world today.

Some historical concepts require us to put on our thinking caps and securely tie them under our chin; this is one of those times. We are about to start a two week study about two men. One was born from disobedience and would always carry and live with the knowledge that he was not the chosen one. This insecurity would taint everything in his life and would become the legacy which was passed from one generation to the next. This man would become the "father" of a world religion that is counter to Christianity. The other man was the chosen one; he was the favored son, the father of the chosen nation. His lineage would lead straight to the cross and the way for forgiveness of all mankind.

In our next chapter, we will learn about Isaac, the chosen son, and his descendants, but for now, I want to spend some time with Ishmael, the son born from disobedience. We, as Christians, need to know the history of Ishmael and his descendants, for it is something that still affects us to this day. Before I start the details of Ishmael's descendants, I would like you to go to the next chapter and study the chart of the genealogy of Abraham. Toward the bottom, there is a long, horizontal line with twelve names on it. These are the twelve sons of a man named Jacob, whom you will learn more about in our next chapter. These are the men that became the "fathers" of the twelve tribes of Israel. What I want you to understand is this: Ishmael also had twelve sons.

Genesis 25:12-17 says,

"12Now these are the generations of Ishmael, Abraham's son, whom Hagar the Egyptian, Sarah's handmaid, bare unto Abraham: 13And these are the names of the sons of Ishmael, by their names, according to their generations: the firstborn of Ishmael, Nebajoth; and Kedar, and Adbeel, and Mibsam, 14And Mishma, and Dumah, and Massa, 15Hadar, and Tema, Jetur, Naphish, and Kedemah: 16These are the sons of Ishmael, and these are their names, by their towns, and by their castles; twelve princes according to their nations. 17And these are the years of the life of Ishmael, an hundred and thirty and seven years: and he gave up the ghost and died; and was gathered unto his people."

As you will learn in our next chapter, Isaac became the grandfather of the twelve sons of Jacob. These tribes became the nation that God had chosen to be the earthly lineage of Jesus Christ, His Son. As you will learn through our study, Satan always tries to counterfeit what God does. The story of

Ishmael and his descendants is an extremely clear picture of this. In fact, I believe it is one of the clearest pictures in the Bible depicting this concept.

Before Ishmael was born, the Lord said this about him (Genesis 16:11-12)

"¹¹And the angel of the LORD said unto her, Behold, thou art with child, and shalt bear a son, and shalt call his name Ishmael; because the LORD hath heard thy affliction. ¹²And he will be a wild man; his hand will be against every man, and every man's hand against him; and he shall dwell in the presence of all his brethren."

I would not want to hear this said about one of my babies, but this is exactly what Ishmael became. As we read in our last chapter's Bible reading, the birth of Ishmael caused much contention between Abraham, Sarah, Hagar, and both of the boys, Ishmael and Isaac. Ishmael and his mother were sent away when Isaac was only a small boy. The Bible makes it clear that Abraham loved Ishmael, and why shouldn't he? Ishmael was his firstborn son. Abraham even begged God to bless Ishmael, but by the time Isaac was old enough to be weaned, probably a toddler, Ishmael was causing trouble. Hagar, Sarah's maid and Ishmael's mother, was sent away, taking her troublesome boy with her.

After Hagar and Ishmael were sent away, they returned to the land of Hagar's people - the land of Egypt. There they settled, and Ishmael married a woman of his mother's choosing, from the maidens of Egypt. This was the beginning of a long string of historical happenings...

Ishmael became the unquestioned leader of the desert peoples throughout the Middle East. His descendants settled near the border of Egypt and became Arabian nomads called Bedouins (BED - o - ins). These people groups all had their own gods and belief systems, some sharing gods and idol worship with their neighbors. In other words, they were not any different than the other nations which worshipped many gods.

The development of their own completely separate belief system happened when a man who history calls Mohammed was born in the year 570 A.D. in the city of Mecca. (Islamic tradition states that Ishmael settled in Mecca.) Ishmael had strong family ties in Africa through both Hagar, his mother, and his wife; both of these important women were Egyptian. Even today, there is a colossal stronghold of Islam in Africa.

Muslims believe that Mohammed started receiving revelations from Allah in the year 610 A.D. They believe that these messages were communicated through the angel Gabriel. Since they could not deny the birth of Christ, the Muslims turned Him into a prophet to explain Him away, and they chose a verse from John 14 to twist for their use. In John 14:16, Jesus tells His followers that He will send a Comforter (or Counselor). We know that He meant the Holy Spirit, the Spirit of Truth (verse 17). They took verse 16 out of context to say the "prophet" Jesus said there would a final prophet coming that would receive the final revelation. Mohammed was called that prophet.

Mohammed's visions are assembled in a book called the Koran, which is alternately spelled "Quran." It is important for us to know how to pronounce these Arabic pronunciations and meanings:

Islam (is-LAM), Allah (al-LAH), and Koran (ko-RON) or Quran (qu-RON). It is also important that, as Christians, we know what makes Islam and Christianity different from each other.

The first important concept to learn is this: we do not share the same God with other religions of the world. Muslims do not believe that Allah is the same as Jehovah. As Christians, we better understand that this is true: Allah and Jehovah are not the same. Please keep your thinking cap on as we work through these differences.

Muslims do not and cannot have a personal relationship with their god. In the Koran, there are ninety-nine names for Allah. Not one of those names is personal or close. There is no part of Allah that is relational. There is a line in the Koran that says threateningly "he is as close as your *jugular." Does that sound like our Jehovah?

While Islam is based on fear and submission, Christianity is entirely based on relationship. We hold the love, grace, and forgiveness of God as the basis for our beliefs. Jahweh is interested in relationships with each of us. This is why He sent His One and only Son to die for our sins. Sin separated us from His presence. He could not stand that, so He made a way for us to come to Him. His yearning to have a relationship with us is the basis of our faith.

So what does this have to do with Ishmael? All believers of Islam may not be actual descendants of Ishmael, but they all consider themselves to be His spiritual descendants. Does this sound familiar? Remember what I said earlier in the chapter about Satan wanting to counterfeit what God does? As Christians, we are the spiritual descendants of Abraham and his son Isaac.

Another contrast between Islam and Christianity is the certainty of what will follow our time here on Earth. First John 5:12-13 says…
"He that hath the Son hath life; and he that hath not the Son of God hath not life. These things have I written to you that believe on the name of the Son of God; that ye may know that ye have eternal life, and that ye may believe on the name of the Son of God."
We can know! We have security! The followers of Islam have no feelings of eternal security. Mohammed said that he did not know where he was going after he died.

The whole of Islamic belief is based on making Ishmael the inheritor of the promise that God gave Abraham concerning Isaac.

Who does Genesis 22 say God told Abraham to place on the altar as a sacrifice? In the Koran, Mohammed changed the Biblical happenings on Mount Moriah from Isaac to Ishmael on the altar. If this was true, than everything that was promised to Isaac would actually go to Ishmael.

The "chapters" of the Koran are called suras. In Sura 112 and 3 it says, "Allah, the Eternal, Absolute; he begetteth not, nor is he begotten." Let's compare this to John 3:16-17. The following words are from Jesus, Himself:
"[16]For God so loved the world, that He gave His only begotten Son, that whosoever believeth in Him should not perish, but have everlasting life. [17]For God sent not His Son into the world to condemn the world; but that the world through Him might be saved."

In Sura 4, it is written that "they killed him not, nor crucified him." If there was no crucifixion, there is no Savior. This is the number one difference between Islam and Christianity.

Read Genesis 16:11-12 and then turn to Genesis 25:18. Compare the two verse segments. What are the similarities? The "he" became a "they." Ishmael's hostility became the hostility that fuels the Islamic religion. Only the good news of our Savior can conquer the darkness of this hostility.

When we read the Bible, right before we read the book of Psalms, we come upon the story of a man named Job. Most people I know do not care very much for this story, and understandably so, because the story is very sad. Even though we do not know the exact dates of the story of Job, we do know that it took place roughly at the same time as Abraham's call and promise from God. Just because it was placed further into the Old Testament line-up of books, doesn't mean that it took place during the life of King David.

It was Job who cried out in yearning for a Mediator Who would plead his case to God. Read Job 9:32-35. It is this longing for a "bridge" or mediator that fills the souls of the world's lost. We must never turn our backs on the lost and hurting, even the Muslim world. Jesus is the Answer for every person who has or ever will draw breath. He is the only One who can heal the broken hearted.

*(A predatory animal often attacks its prey by biting this major vein in the neck of its victim.)

Narration Break: Discuss the last part of our chapter.

Chapter 9

Islamic Raiders Take Spain

In our last chapter, we learned about how the Islamic Empire was stretching its long, powerful arms out of the Arabian Peninsula and up into Europe and Asia. Several chapter ago, we learned about how China, India, and Japan all were united by one strong leader. In this chapter, we are going to learn about how several Barbarian tribes were also united under one strong leader.

You will remember that it was the Huns, who destroyed Rome. Other Barbarian tribes had settled in the area, which is now France and parts of Spain, but in those days, was called Gaul. In many ways, these tribes had adopted the Roman way of doing things and did not consider themselves to be "Barbarian" anymore. Even though these tribes did not like each other, they liked the Huns even less. One of the tribes, the Franks, had a strong leader, who was able to unite all of the tribes in the region. This Frankish leader's name was Merovius, and he was able to defeat the invading Huns. Unfortunately, after the crisis, they all went back to fighting amongst themselves.

In the year 481, Merovius's grandson, Clovis, inherited his tribe's throne. Clovis remembered how his grandfather had united the tribes of Gaul long enough to fight against the Huns. He was determined to permanently unite them, and then to become king of them all, so he devised a plan.

Chapter 9

First, he married a princess of the neighboring tribe, the Burgundians. His new wife, Clotilda, was a Christian, and she wanted Clovis to become a Christian, too, but Clovis did not want to become a Christian, but he did not want to convert.

Legend says that one day, Clovis was fighting a battle against the Allemani tribe in northern Gaul. His army was doing very poorly and sustaining heavy casualties. Clovis looked up to the sky and told God that he would serve Him forever if He would give the Frankish army the victory. The legend goes on to say that the army's energy and strength was miraculously revived, and they went on to win the battle with renewed vigor. After the battle was over, Clovis returned home to speak to a priest about Christianity and to be baptized. He was now an emperor of his new kingdom and a Christian.

The new Frankish Empire now ruled all of Gaul, with Clovis as their king. (We get the word "France" from the word "Frank.") Now that Clovis had conquered everyone and united the empire, he had to devise a plan to keep them united. He decided that having a common religion would help, so he decreed his empire would be a "Christian Empire." When he was baptized into the church, he ordered over three thousand of his men to be baptized, too. Of course, being baptized does not make you a Christian, but in Clovis's mind, it did.

Clovis also decided that he needed to come up with strict laws that everyone had to follow. (His new set of laws reminds me somewhat of Hammurabi's Code!) Up until now, all of the tribes had followed their own laws, and Clovis knew if this continued, there would be too much division to keep his empire united. So Clovis ordered his scribes to write down his new set of laws, which he called the Salic Laws.

Narration Break: Find the location of the events in this chapter on your world map and narrate the story of how Clovis became king of Gaul.

The Frankish Empire continued to grow strong, united under their national religion and following their universal law. To the west of the Frankish empire, there was another ex-Barbarian tribe. Like the Franks, the Visigoths had been what I like to call, un-holy terrors! Their pillaging and plundering ways struck terror in the hearts of many civilizations and empires of the ancient world. Like the Franks, however, the Visigoths had settled down and adopted a civilized way of life. The Visigoths' culture had been greatly influenced by the Romans. Also, like the Franks, the Visigoths considered themselves to be a Christian empire. Everything was going along uneventfully for them until their king died unexpectedly.

Following the king's death, there was a civil war over who should be the Visigoths' next ruler. Some people believed that the natural choice would be one of the king's sons, while others wanted a man named Rodrigo to rule the kingdom. Rodrigo, they argued, would be a better ruler because he was a famous and highly feared warrior. Who would dare mess with the Visigoths if such a ruler was on the throne? And so, it was settled; Rodrigo was crowned king. This, of course, angered the sons of the dead king, and they swore that they would not give over their rights to the crown.

The sons gathered together and hatched a scheme; they would ask a great warrior from North Africa to come and help them regain power over their kingdom. This scheme was destined to end in disaster, though. The North African warrior, Tariq Bin Ziyad, was a Muslim commander. You will remember from our last chapter that the Muslims wanted to spread their religion everywhere. Since the events in Chapter 8, the Muslims had spread far and wide, and they had built up their army in Northern Africa to twelve thousand strong. These warriors were called Berbers, and Tariq bin Ziyad was one of their leaders.

When Tariq bin Ziyad received an invitation to cross the water of what is now called the Strait of Gibraltar and come into Spain, he was more than happy to oblige. Oh, he had no intention whatsoever of helping the king's sons! He wanted to capture Spain for Islam. The Visigoths, who were divided by the dispute for the throne, were not able to ward off the Islamic raiders' attack, and soon, Spain was completely under Tariq bin Ziyad's control. The name Gibraltar

comes from the words, "Jabal Tariq," which means the "mountain of Tariq." The rocky hill, upon which Tariq stood to command his troops to come ashore, is still to this day, called the rock of Gibraltar.

As the Islamic reign spread throughout Spain, the Franks watched nervously from the East. Everyone knew the Muslim army was a powerful force with which to reckon. The serge of Islamic victories was something of a tidal wave, wiping away everything in its path. Their warriors believed that their god,

Allah, would not let them be defeated. However, they were about to meet someone who would do just that!

By this time, in the Frankish empire, there was a king like none other. This king was so mighty that people called him "Charles Martel." The word, "Martel," means "the Hammer." Charles had not gotten to be king easily; he

had "scratched and clawed" his way to the throne. There were many people who did not want him to become king, and they threw him into prison. Charles did not let this stop him, however. He escaped, gathered his army, and fought those who opposed his being king. Now, he was facing the most feared army in the world at that time.

The Muslim raiders thought they would sweep through

France the same way they had conquered Spain. At first, it appeared they would do exactly this because they pillaged and plundered the small villages and towns all along the border. After Tariq bin Ziyad and his men had become so laden down with plunder that they could hardly move, they met the Hammer!

When the Islamic warriors approached, Charles Martel gathered his army together to meet them. The Muslim raiders met Charles Martel's army at the city of Tours. The Muslims, expecting an easy victory, were stunned by the strength of the Frankish army. Charles Martel drove his army hard, forcing the Islamic raiders to run and flee. The Islamic tidal wave had been stopped.

Narration Break: Tell the story of Tariq bin Ziyad. What happened when he met Charles the Hammer?

Chapter 10

The Story of Charlemagne

Before we move to the main topic of our chapter, I want to tell you about something that happened in the early church. We have learned that, although we may wish to separate world history and church history of this time period, sometimes that is not possible. We have also learned that the church and government became united under the rule of Constantine.

The rise of Islam brought with it numerous areas of discussion and, many times, disagreement. One of these topics of disagreement started when the Muslims called the Christians "idol-worshippers." Why would they call them this? The early church had many statues and images of Jesus and the apostles, and it was a common practice to show respect by kissing them. The Muslims' accusations caused many Christians to stop and question this practice. Was kissing these statues dishonoring to God?

When a volcano disturbed Constantinople in AD 725, people feared it was God showing His anger against this practice of image kissing. A major controversy was unfolding in the church. Those who kissed the statues and paintings of Jesus or the "saints" were called "Icondules," which means "Icon-kissers."

The Byzantine emperor thought if he got rid of the icons, the trouble would be over, and his kingdom would be more peaceful once again. With this intent, he sent soldiers to smash a huge golden statue of Christ, which stood above the palace door. However, the angry crowd would not let the soldiers near the statue. The people started calling the emperor and those who agreed with him, "Icon-smashers" or "Iconoclast."

The matter was finally settled by more than three hundred fifty church overseers, who gathered in Nicaea. They denounced the smashers but banned icon-worship. They tried to find a common ground by promoting what they called "icon reverence."

The church, by this time, was divided geographically. The Church, in the region that once was the Western Roman Empire, was called the Roman Church. (The Frankish kings were part of this section of the church.) The Church in the other section was the Eastern Church, which was centered in the great city of Constantinople, in the Byzantine Empire. In the year 754, the Frankish king, Pepin III, the son of Charles Martel, gave the Roman church a very generous gift - most of central Italy. The church was gaining power!

Both the church and the emperors of the Frankish and Byzantine empires benefitted from their relationship. Having the church's blessing helped the king to be more respected, while the church enjoyed more freedom and vast wealth. When Pepin died in 768, he left the Frankish throne to his sons, Carloman and Charles. When Carloman died in 771, Charles inherited his brother's portion of the kingdom. Charles was a great military leader, who had his heart set on conquering the surrounding lands.

Charles was also concerned about the people of his empire. He worried that they were slowly returning to their old, barbarian ways and that they were forgetting how to be Christians. Charles decided to hire hundreds of monks to copy the Scriptures by hand in order to supply even the most rural village

The Empire of Charlemagne

Scottish Kingdoms

Irish Kingdom

England

Paris

Frankish Empire

Slavs

Rome

churches with Bibles. He commanded that all children be baptized and brought to church. Charles looked around and decided that his kingdom needed to be cleaned up and the road systems repaired.

All of this renovating effort and conquering of the surrounding lands went on for thirty years until Charles was the ruler of a huge empire. He rebuilt old Roman roads, rebuilt old Roman structures, and built new buildings with the flair of old Roman architecture. Everywhere he went, Charles conquered "in the name of God." In a very unChristian manner, he forced all of his people to be baptized or die.

To the south, a group of Italian lords were trying to take over the Roman church. They captured and tortured the Roman church overseer, Pope Leo III. They accused him of stealing from the church, and they cut out his tongue. This, of course, made it impossible to speak to defend himself. The Italian lords then took Pope Leo III to Emperor Charles. They demanded that the pope be removed from his office. Their plan failed, however, because Charles

and Leo decide to help each other. Charles declared Leo innocent of the charges, and in return, Leo would give Charles a public blessing.

Two days later, at the Christmas Day communion service, Leo III crowned King Charles, "Charles Augustus, crowned by God as supreme and peaceful Emperor." Charles, the Frankish king, had become Charlemagne, the Holy Roman Emperor. Charlemagne had revived the hope for a renewed Western Roman Empire and saved the church from the greedy Italian lords.

Narration Break: Narrate the story of "icon-kissers" and "icon-smashers." Tell about Charlemagne."

Chapter 10

Do you remember how the Roman Empire became big and strong? The Roman citizens thought their empire was indestructible. Do you remember what happened? Barbarian tribes started invading the border towns and villages, effectively whittling away at the seemingly impregnable Roman Empire. We all know what became of the empire and how it finally fell.

As Charlemagne basked in the glow of his new title and the adoration of his citizens, he thought to himself that he had built a kingdom second only to the original Roman Empire. Surely nothing would ever make his kingdom collapse into a dusty heap like the Roman Empire had! While Charlemagne was on the throne, his army was well-organized, and no attacking tribes were successful at breaking into his kingdom. After his death, however, the kingdom was divided between his three grandsons. We know from studying history, that when a kingdom or an empire is divided between more than one ruler, trouble usually follows, and of course, this was the case with the Frankish Empire.

After the division of the kingdom, the Frankish army wasn't as strong, and the invading tribes from the North were able to break through and conquer sections of the empire. Some of these invaders were warriors from the Scandinavian Peninsula. They came from the kingdoms of Norway, Sweden, and Denmark, and were North-men or Norsemen. Study the map below.

Our name for these people comes from their own word for adventuring. When they were about to go out for one of their raids, on one of their neighbors, they said they were going "i viking." Soon, this is what they were commonly called. The Vikings started venturing further away from their lands

in the north during the 700s, because they were in search for better farmlands. These men were excellent boat and ship makers, and they made special ships that were designed to ride through shallow water. These Viking ships are still admired worldwide for their uniqueness and versatility.

At first, the Vikings raided the border villages and the rich monasteries, but they soon became bolder, venturing further and further inland. The Vikings, using their amazing ships down the River Rhine in Germany and the Sine River in France, attacked France after Charlemagne had died. They knew that the three grandsons were busier keeping their eye on each other, rather than keeping their eye on their kingdom.

In 911, the king of France gave the Vikings the province of Normandy in which to settle. He thought if he gave them their own land, maybe they would stop their looting and pillaging. Soon, the Vikings were calling themselves

"Normans," and it was as Normans they attacked England in the north in 1066, and in the 1070s, Italy and Sicily. The Normans also traveled up into Iceland, Greenland, and North America, many of them settling as they traveled.

The Vikings had an enormous impact on the future of huge areas, if not all, of Northern Europe. Even Russia suffered from the Viking's attacks. The Vikings invaded countries all along the Mediterranean Sea coast, but when they attacked

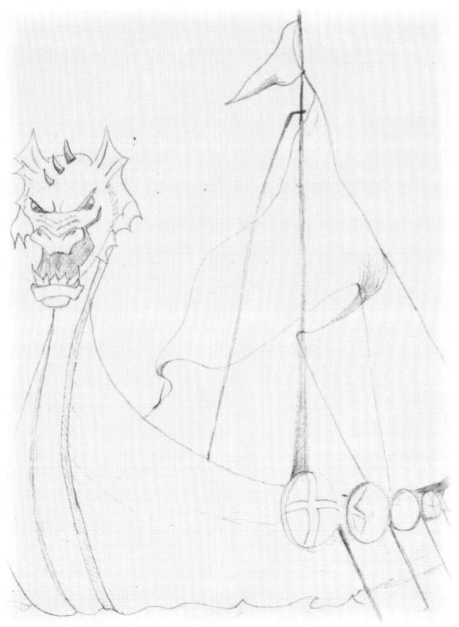

Byzantium, they soon found they were no match for the well-trained armies there.

The Vikings had a positive impact on the world, too. They were responsible for establishing trade routes, founding towns throughout Russia, and greatly influencing the cultures and trades of Britain, France, Poland, and even Ireland. So, whether by invasion or by settling, the Vikings left their mark all over Europe and Asia.

If you have read Volume 1 of this history series, you will no doubt remember the story of a Viking named Eric and his son, Leif. Eric, who was called "Eric the Red," partly because of his wild, bright red hair, but mostly because of his wild, crazy temper, was forced to leave their home in Iceland (which, ironically is very green!) and move to Greenland. Greenland is covered in ice. With the exception of a narrow strip along the coastline, Greenland is a huge "disk" of ice.

It is Leif, who is credited for discovering the continent of North American around the year 1000. Even though the account of this discovery was not widely believed until almost five hundred years later, the tale of this new land was passed down through legends told around the Vikings' fires.

Narration Break: <u>Narrate the last section of the chapter.</u>

Chapter 11

Alfred the Great & William the Conquerer

(And other interesting happenings of the time...)

Please study this map of Britain. We learned, in our last chapter, about the Vikings roamed about Europe and Asia, pillaging and conquering nations everywhere. When the Vikings who moved into France, settled down, they became known as the Normans. Next, these Normans invaded Britain to their north.

Chapter 11

We have learned about Britain and how the Celts had lived there. The Celts had lived there for so long, in fact, that back in Jesus' day, the Romans had tried to take over and extend their empire all the way to the tip of the British Isles. Next, the Celts endured raids from Barbarian tribes from the North. When the Anglo-Saxons, as they had come to be called, settled in and became Britons, some Celts went north into Scotland and Ireland.

Now, when the Vikings-turned-Normans arrived in Britain, the Celts and the Anglo-Saxons were terrified! Word of these ruthless invaders had spread far and wide, and accounts of the pillaging and plundering struck fear in the hearts of even the toughest, strongest people. At this time in Britain, there was not a strong king on the throne ruling everyone. Britain had been divided into seven smaller kingdoms. When the Viking-Normans swept into Britain, they burned everything they came across. They were not Christians, and they had no respect for the church, so they pillaged and plundered the monasteries. (In the next section of this chapter, we will learn the importance of these

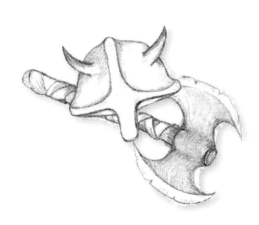

monasteries to the culture of the world.) These uncouth people stole the images, ornate fixtures, and precious metal and wood from the churches.

Once the Vikings settled into their new home after conquering large sections of Britain, they invited relatives and friends, in Scandinavia, to come and visit and even settle near them. Swarms of Vikings answered this invitation and soon all of central England was under Viking control.

Chapter 11

Next, Vikings moved over into Ireland. They conquered the people and took over all of the fertile farmland and settled there. Now that they controlled so much of England and Ireland, the Viking leaders decided to go down into Southern England. Why not try to rule all of Britain? The leaders of the Vikings, two brothers named Halfdan and Ivar the Boneless (apparently they were extremely tall and thin), did not know about the ruler of Wessex, the most southern kingdom in England.

Halfdan sent one of his mightiest commanders to invade Wessex. The people of Wessex tried to pay the Viking invaders off, but that plan did not work well.. The citizens of Wessex concluded that they needed to have a strong leader, who could stand against Guthrum, the Viking commander. They chose a brave nobleman named Alfred.

Alfred hid from the invading Guthrum and his army in order to gather an army and enough ammunition to defend Wessex. They met the Viking army and beat them so badly that the Vikings were forced to hide in a castle. Alfred and his army surrounded the castle and starved the Vikings into surrender. Thus ended the Viking run of victory through England. They returned north and left the Wessex citizens alone. Alfred became known as Alfred the Great.

After Alfred the Great, the English kept having to fight off the Vikings. Things went well for awhile; Alfred's son, Edward, was a powerful ruler, who conquered some of the areas north of Wessex and defeated the Vikings. However, the kings who followed were weak and unable to defend England.

Chapter 11

In the year 1013, one of Alfred's descendants, Ethlred, was defeated by the Viking king living in England. After that, the Vikings ruled England for many years, and their distinct cultures began to blend. Vikings, Celts, and English lived side by side, married each other, and accepted each others' traditions. Life went along for awhile until a ruler had to be chosen to follow King Edward, because he had no heir. Of course, there was a great argument about who should become the next ruler of England. Most people wanted a nobleman, who was from Wessex like Alfred the Great. One nobleman from Wessex, Harold, was a good leader, and it seemed that he was the most logical choice.

However, as is the case most of the time in situations like this, someone else thought that they could do a better job and that they were the true heir to the throne. Edward, the last king, had a distant, half-French cousin living in Normandy, who believed that he should be the next king of England. William the Norman was not even an Englishman, but he devised a plan to become the ruler of England. There are varying accounts of what happened next but we do know that William tricked Harold into promising to hand over the crown of England. There was a huge battle, which became one of the most famous battles in the history of England. The Battle of Hastings ended with the death of Harold and the invasion of the French-speaking Normans. Another people group now moved into England, bringing with them their language and their foreign customs and cultures.

Narration Break: Narrate the story of how the Viking/Normans came to be in England.

Chapter 11

Do you remember when we learned about the Feudal System back in Chapter 7? In that chapter, we painted a back drop of sorts showing the general lifestyle of the Middle Ages. Of course, not everyone lived in castles. some people lived on farms or in small villages with large commons in the center. These commons were large, grassy areas where everyone kept their livestock. This is the way the English had lived for many years, but after the Normans invaded, and William, who became William the Conquerer, became king, life changed in England.

The Normans brought with them their way of life and thought; since they now ruled the land, they owned it - ALL of it. William came to the conclusion that he had the right to take the land and divide it amongst his generals and lords. Do you remember the lords of the Feudal System? They owned large areas of land (or in some cases, they only governed land owned by the king), and they had many, many people working for them. These citizens, the farmers, merchants, and villagers, not only worked for these lords, they also paid heavy taxes to fund building projects that the king or the lord wanted completed. These people were called serfs, and they were at the mercy of the king and the temperament of the lord.

The cultural climate was rather dark and dreary. Many serfs worked hard all of their lives without ever making a better living standard for their family. Education was rare, and hope seemed to be fading. It was during this time that many depended on the church for help. Throughout England as well as many other countries of Europe, there were places of help and outreach. These were the monasteries and convents, where many monks and nuns lived their lives to help those in need around them. They were truly lights in the darkness. Even though there was trouble in the church at large, individuals who followed Jesus made a huge difference in the world around them.

Monasteries and convents were safe-houses for those in need. Hundreds of monks worked to handwrite books and supply village churches with religious literature. Nuns worked to teach their neighbors better gardening techniques, cared for the ill, and raised orphans.

The years between 880-980 were dark years for the church, just as they were dark for the rest of the world. The church and the government were intertwined by this time, and both had suffered from years of corrupt leadership. The position of the pope had fallen into the hands of a series of evil nobles, and an Italian heiress, named Morazia (mor-OZ-ee-uh), manipulated the bishops of Rome for over sixty years! In 955, Marozia's grandson, Pope Jone XII, celebrated his election as pope with a toast to the devil. What was going on? How could the Christian church go so far down the wrong path? A storm was coming, though! I think God might have seen the need for a sifting

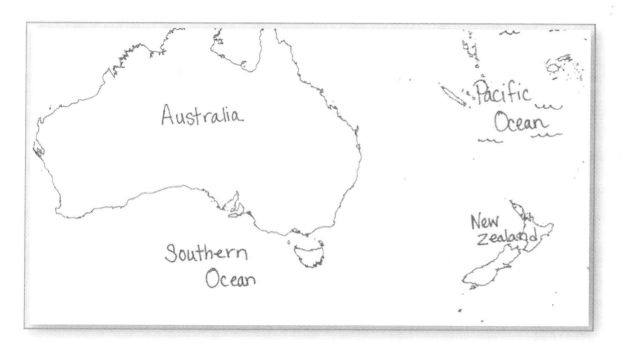

of His church. Three heavy blows, which we will learn about soon, were coming to the church to start this process. [2]

For the rest of our chapter, we are going to leave the crowded landscape of Europe and take a little trip to the southeast. In fact, why don't we pause and fetch a globe? We have been spending a vast amount of time up in the Northern Hemisphere, in Europe and Asia. Let's start by finding Europe on the globe. Do you see England, France, and the Scandinavian Peninsula? Travel with your finger east toward Russia and China. Now drop straight south until you reach Australia. Right below and to the east of Australia are two large islands. This is New Zealand. Take a moment and look at all of the islands scattered here and there throughout this area. This is called Oceania.

No one knows for sure exactly from where the first inhabitants of New Zealand came, but most historians think they migrated from Taiwan down to the Philippines, then to the islands in the Pacific and the Bismarck Sea, and eventually down to New Zealand and the surrounding islands.

The people of Australia and the surrounding islands were nomadic for many centuries. They traveled around looking for food and shelter, often choosing certain locations to cope with the climate. The original inhabitants of this area are called Aborigines, which comes from the words, "from the beginning." As far as anyone knows, these people have always lived in Australia. Perhaps they have even lived in this area since the dispersion after the Tower of Babel.

Chapter 11

Unlike the Aborigines of Australia, the Maori, who were the first real inhabitants of New Zealand, came there during the Middle Ages. These people are thought to be Polynesians. This means that they were from the Polynesian Islands, a huge group of islands scattered far and wide in the Pacific Ocean, between Australia and the Americas.

The Polynesians were great navigators. They embarked on many discovery adventures, with their boats made from giant logs. These boats were really more like giant canoes, with sails made from woven material. This is how these people came to New Zealand. They brought livestock and food and came ashore looking for a good place to live.

The Polynesians not only traveled to New Zealand and other other islands around Australia; they also traveled all the way to the Americas! Here, they traded with the natives and brought back with them new foods, such as sweet potatoes. The Polynesians' way of life was isolated from the rest of Europe and Asia, and therefore, influences from other civilizations did not come until much later. The Maori grew in number and split into tribes. Some of them were more peaceful people and settled down to farm, while others were more prone to fighting. These fighting tribes became the warriors of the Maori people.

You many have seen pictures of these huge statues that are on Easter Island in Polynesia. There are more than five hundred of these fifty-ton statues on this island. No one is sure who carved them or for what purpose, but most historians agree that the statues were used as part of religious ceremonies. The statues are carved from volcanic rock and are extremely old. They are thought to date back to the time before the Polynesians came to that island.

Narration Break: Discuss the last part of the chapter.

Chapter 12

The Early Crusades & The Jews of the Middle Ages

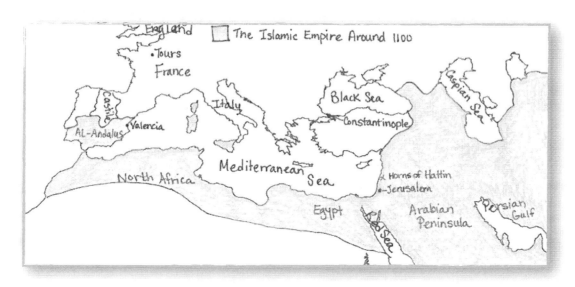

You will remember that the Muslims had swarmed out from their original home on the Arabian Peninsula, gathering in strength and in number as they marched through the land. We learned, in Chapter 9, how Muslim raiders took over Spain and then tried to conquer France. Islamic forces had also conquered and had been in control of the Jewish Holy city, Jerusalem, since about the year 638.

In Medieval times, the Christians believed that everyone should make a pilgrimage to Jerusalem, at least once, at some point in their lives. They thought they could show their desire to turn from sin by going on this ultimate pilgrimage. Although the Muslims had controlled Jerusalem and all of the surrounding roads for many years, they had allowed the Christians to travel without much interference. Eventually, there was trouble; the Muslims started charging traveling taxes or tariffs. These Muslims were known as Turks, and they harassed the Christian pilgrims unmercifully.

This mistreatment went on until the Christians' pilgrimages to Jerusalem had all but stopped. In 1095, Pope Urban II addressed the issue by preaching one of history's most influential sermons.

"Your Eastern brothers have asked for your help! Turks and Arabs have conquered their territories. I - or, rather, the Lord - beg you... destroy that vile race from their lands!" [3]

It is doubtful that Pope Urban II thought he would get the response that followed. The astounded pope watched as the crowd began to scream and chant, "God wills it!" From every direction, men gathered together. Lords, ruffians, and serfs all swore to fight together in order to " drive the infidels from the face of the earth."

These men sewed red crosses on their tunics and became "Crusaders," - soldiers of the cross. While the Crusaders trained and readied themselves for battle with the Muslims, something else was happening. A monk, called Peter the Hermit, was gathering many of the common-folk together. He told them that everyone had a right, and indeed, the obligation to run the Muslims off of the face of the earth.

This Peter was a rather interesting person; he was well-known for his loathing of the bathtub and was quite a dirty, smelly man. He was also known to ride his donkey, while wearing a dirty, brown, monk's cloak. People jokingly commented that he and his donkey resembled each other, with their brown coats and long faces.

Thousands of people followed Peter the Hermit, even though most of them never fought the Muslims. Instead, many of them turned into a rather wild, hungry mob, whom Peter deserted to find safety. This strange occurrence became known as the People's Crusade, even though nothing Crusade-like ever came from it.

It was in 1099, when a well organized and trained army of Crusaders marched toward Jerusalem. There they recaptured the city. I am not going to go into the details of all that happened there that day. No words can express the horrors committed in the name of Christianity. Instead of trying to find a way to express God's love to the lost, those who claimed to follow Christ chose to kill them instead. This is a very dark time in history, and one that is extremely hard to write about, but as we have learned, we cannot learn from history unless we learn about history. This was the first Crusade.

After the Crusaders captured Jerusalem, they established four "states" in Palestine and Syria. For a while, everyone seemed to settle down a bit, as Crusader generals and nobles established a form of feudalism over the conquered lands and built Norman-style castles and estates. The Muslims left the Crusaders' kingdoms alone for eighty-nine years, and then everything changed. A Muslim captain, named Saladin, who had strategically worked his way up through the ranks of the Islamic army, headed toward Jerusalem. Saladin dreamed and planned all of his life for this venture.

News of his approach struck fear in the hearts of the Crusader king of Jerusalem. He gathered his advisors and asked them what he should do - should he go down and face the approaching enemy, or should he stay and fight the Islamic attack from behind the city walls? Some of his advisors implored him to stay in safety and allow the invading army to do the work of climbing up to the city. Others told him that they should be fearless and go down to meet Saladin.

The king decided to go and attack the oncoming army, but he did not take the hot, summer weather into consideration. The Crusader army was so extremely hot and thirsty, they could do nothing but lay in their tents and suffer from heat exhaustion. There was not even a battle; Saladin simply came with his men, surrounded their camp, and captured them. Jerusalem was once again under Islamic control. Saladin was now king of Jerusalem, and because he wanted to prove to the world that he was a different kind of Muslim, he declared that the Christians and Jews would be able to visit the Holy City unhindered.

Narration Break: Narrate the story of the First and Second Crusade.

With all of this talk about the fighting over Jerusalem, you might be wondering where the Jews were during all of this. After all, they were the ones who had built the city! If you have studied Volume 4 of this series, you will remember the story of Abraham and how God told him leave his home in

Ur to travel to a land He would show him. There, God promised to make Abraham the father of a great nation, with more offspring than he could count. Hebrews 11 tells us that Abraham obeyed God, and that his obedience was credited to him as faith. Abraham was not perfect in his obedience, as we learned earlier, and his impatience with waiting for the son God had promised has caused a lot of problems in the world. From his disobedience, Ishmael was brought into the world. It was from Isaac, the chosen son of Abraham, that God brought forth His chosen nation, the Jews. These people were sometimes very disobedient and just like us, had to be disciplined.

God was patient with His people, though, and did eventually choose a young, unmarried, Jewish girl to be the earthly mother of His Son, Jesus. We learned earlier in this volume that the Romans were occupying Israel at the time of Christ. It was not even that many years after Christ had died, been resurrected, and returned to His place by His Father's right hand, that the Romans had brought their heavy hand down on the Jewish people. They destroyed the Temple and dispersed the Jewish nation.

There is a word we use to describe this scattering of the Jews among the nations of the world, and this word is the Diaspora. The Diaspora was complete when Jerusalem was desecrated, the Temple destroyed and the Jews disbanded in the year AD 70. This caused a major problem for the Jews. If they left Israel and Jerusalem, they would no longer have the one identifying element that held them all together - worship in the Temple. They would have to intentionally focus on maintaining their identity as Jews. Remember, now that Jesus had come and fulfilled the Old Testament prophecies, there were those who followed His teachings and believed that He was the Messiah - the Lamb of God and the Savior of the world. On the other hand, there were the

Jews who did not believe Jesus is the Messiah. These are the Orthodox Jews, and their holy book is the Torah. In essence, the Torah is the first five books of the Old Testament (these are the books of the law).

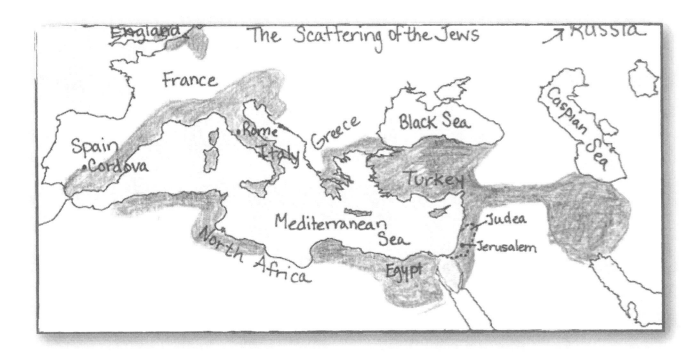

After the Diaspora, the Jews scattered far and wide, taking up residence in almost every country of the world. Wherever they lived, though, they remained first and foremost, Jews. Their religion was their identity. The Jews are perhaps the most persecuted people group in the history of the world. Everywhere they settled, they were misunderstood and, many times, mistreated. Even though they learned the language and way of life of the country in which they settled, the Jews kept themselves separate. Their way of worshipping God made people suspicious of them. The Jews were so different, in fact, that both England and France would not let them settle in their countries during the Middle Ages.

Chapter 12

The scattered Jews divided into three distinct geographical groups. Those who emigrated to Central and Eastern Europe were called Ashkenazi Jews. Those who settled in Iberia and North Africa were the Sephardi Jews, and the group that remained in the Babylon area after the first Temple was destroyed (586 BC), are called the Mizrahi Jews. During the twentieth century, millions of Jews from all three geographical groups emigrated to the United States.

Narration Break: Discuss the last part of the chapter.

Chapter 13

Richard the Lionhearted, John Lackland, and other Legendary Events

The protagonists of this chapter are perhaps some of the most well-known characters of all the Middle Ages. In fact, when one thinks of this time period in history, besides images of castles, Richard the Lionhearted and Robin Hood most likely come to mind. In this chapter, we will explore the true stories behind these famous characters. Many times famous, much-admired, historical figures begin to cast larger-than-life shadows on the walls of the imagination. Such is the case of Richard the Lionhearted, his brother, John, and Robin Hood, that rascal who lived in Sherwood Forest with his band of Merry Men.

First, let us meet Richard the Lionhearted. Unlike King Arthur, Richard was most certainly a real person in history. He was the second son of Henry II of England and Eleanor of Aquitaine, France. After his parents separated, ten year old Richard lived with his mother in Aquitaine, where she schooled him in the arts of reading, writing, and languages. Richard was also trained for knighthood. Richard was a splendid knight in training. He made quite the handsome figure, with his broad shoulders, blonde hair, and tall frame. Many people admired this young prince, who seemed, from the start, to be destined for great things. In 1172, Richard became Duke of Aquitaine and swore his allegiance to the king of France.

When Richard became a duke, he really did not gain any power. Of course this made Richard and his brothers, who had also been given titles, very unhappy. What good was having a title with no power or authority? Richard and his father feuded about this for several years. In the end, Richard asked his father for forgiveness, and his father gave him more responsibility and authority. When Richard was twenty-five, his older brother died, making Richard the heir to the English throne.

Four years later, news traveled from Jerusalem that Saladin, the Muslim raider, had attacked and conquered the Holy City. Richard immediately began planning on becoming a Crusader and leading an army to retake Jerusalem. While Richard was still in the preparation stages of becoming a crusader, he received the terrible news of his father's death. Richard was now the king of England. (It is interesting to note that Richard was the only English king who could not speak English!)

When Richard arrived in England for his coronation, excited crowds filled the streets. This tall, handsome man was exactly what everyone believed a knight and a king should look like! His reputation for bravery and intelligence preceded him, and his kingly presence caused adoration and allegiance from his subjects. As king, Richard sold England's high political positions to the highest bidder to gather money for his crusade; he was still intent upon reconquering Jerusalem. Next, he freed all of the "forest outlaws," who were men caught poaching. This pardon made Richard popular with the common people of England.

After he had taken care of his kingly business, Richard departed on his long-awaited crusade. The journey toward Jerusalem was tedious and had many snags. On his voyage across the Mediterranean Sea, Richard stopped at Sicily to rescue his sister, Joan, who was being held captive there. She had been married to the Sicilian king until he died, and now the new king would not allow her to leave.

Chapter 13

While he was in Sicily, Richard became betrothed to a princess from the Spanish kingdom of Navarre. This did not make a certain, young lady in France very happy! You see, Richard had been betrothed to Princess Alice of France since they were both children. Alice's father, King Philip of France, didn't like the news of Richard's new betrothal either, and he decided to make Richard pay for it.

After some difficulty with his ships and crews, Richard and his men finally arrived in the Holy Land. Here they joined several other groups of Crusaders, led by a duke of Austria and the king of France. Neither of these men liked Richard, each for their own reason. The king of France took his men and went home because he was unwilling to listen to Richard. The Austrian duke refused to fly his banners lower than Richard's, out of respect for his political rank. So Richard commanded his men to steal the banner and trample it in the mud. This insulted the Austrian Duke so much that he swore his hatred of Richard, took his men, and went home. Richard was left with only his own army to attack the Muslims in Jerusalem and the mighty Saladin.

Several times during the Crusade, Richard was close enough to attack Jerusalem, but his knowledge of war tactics kept him from doing so. He knew that he and his men would suffer heavy casualties and would not be able to hold off the waves of Muslim armed forces that would surely attack from the south. Saladin, himself, admired Richard's intelligence, and the two men made an agreement that Saladin would not attack any of the fortresses and provinces currently being held by the crusaders.

It was during this time that Richard received news saying that his younger brother, John, was trying to take over the English throne, and Richard decided that it was time for him to return home. His return trip was as marked by peril as his earlier journey to the Holy Land. Richard was kidnapped by his sworn foe, the Austrian duke, as he passed through that area. (He had been forced to take that route because he had to avoid the angry king of France, Phillip II.) Richard was locked away, in a prison tower, for so long that he was presumed dead.

There are few recorded facts about his captivity and rescue, but there are plenty of legends! One of these legends says that Richard heard a traveling minstrel whistling the English song, *Greensleeves,* under the tower's window. Richard leaned from the tower and whistled the second verse. The minstrel saw Richard in the window and heard him whistling the tune. In great excitement, the minstrel returned home to England to proclaim that their beloved king was indeed alive!

The people of England rushed to raise a ransom in order to free their favorite king. Prince John and his loyal men fought and sabotaged their attempts at every turn. Eventually, Richard did return to England and his throne. Some accounts of this story say the brothers, Richard and John, did not like each other, while other accounts state that Richard was actually quite fond of his little brother. At any rate, Richard pardoned his brother of his treasonous acts.

Richard did not stay in England very long. Soon, he was off to France to fight for lands that he claimed were rightfully his. It was here, while he was fighting to conquer a little French castle, that Richard the Lionhearted was struck by an arrow. It really wasn't a horrible wound, but it became infected and proved to be the demise of the great king. King Richard died and left the English throne to his brother, John.

Narration Break: <u>Narrate the story of Richard the Lionhearted.</u>

I think it is rather strange how King Richard was called the Lionhearted. His brother John, the brother who tried to steal the crown, did not have such a glamorous name, however. When Richard inherited the crown of England, he inherited all of the land of England. Remember, in the Feudal System, the king of a country owned all of the land. He appointed his officers and nobles sections of land to govern, but the king was considered to be the true land owner.

Although Richard owned a vast amount of land, his brother, John did not own any land. He became known as John Lackland because of this. Even when Richard died, and John became king, he was still called John Lackland! John not only had an annoying name; he also had many other troubles. For one, nobody took him very seriously. Richard had treated him like a child when the ransom had set him free. Besides nobody taking him seriously, John did not look the part like his brother had. Instead, he was short, plump, and balding. He certainly did not make the same impression as Richard had!

John decided he was going to make people take him seriously, so he set out to become a tough guy. The French had been trying to take over some of the English castles in France, so John decided to use this excuse to go to war with France. He fought and fought but did not seem to get anywhere. All of these battles with the French cost a lot of money, so he had to think of some creative ways to raise the funds. One of his worst fundraising tactics was a special tax, which he imposed on his noblemen. When this didn't bring enough funds in fast enough, he imposed an inheritance tax. This tax was imposed when a nobleman died; his son, who inherited the estate, was taxed with extremely heavy fees. The situation was even worse if the son was a child. King John became the part owner of the estate and took much more. All of this fighting with France and taxing of his people made John extremely unpopular!

The noblemen became so angry that they gathered their own army, marched on London, and captured it. I suppose these men were tired of the king being above the law. Why should they be taxed to fund battles being fought to make an insecure king feel better about himself? They decided that the law should be the highest power in the land. The law should even be above the king. In 1215, the noblemen, who had captured London, met in a field called Runnymede. King John, knowing that he was extremely unpopular and far outnumbered, realized there was no way for him to recapture London. He dressed in his royal attire and went down to Runnymede to talk to the nobles.

The nobles had drawn up an agreement which they demanded that he sign. This agreement stated that he, the king, and all the following kings, were absolutely required to follow the law of the land in the same way everyone else was required to. This agreement also stated that the king could not throw the nobles or anyone else into jail unless they had been convicted of a crime. Of course, King John did not want to sign the agreement, but he knew that these nobles meant business.

This agreement was called the "Great Charter" or the "Magna Carta." It was an extremely important event, not only for England, but for the whole world. It started the movement of the government of mankind, from the shadows of tyranny and dictatorship, to a more fair and balanced government. No longer would rulers be followed and obeyed blindly. From then on, if the king wanted to make a major decision that affected the whole nation, he had to gain the approval of a group of elected representatives. This was the beginning of the parliament system, and it started to bring the Feudal System to an end.

Narration Break: Narrate the story of John Lackland. What was the Magna Carta?

Chapter 14

A Look at Ireland & the Mighty Genghis Kahn
(and Other Interesting Events)

In our last few chapters, we have been learning about the happenings of Europe during the twelfth century. It might seem that Europe and parts of Asia were the only places where anything ever happened, but of course, events were happening all over the world, just as they do now. We must not think of history as a stage play, with only the actors in the spotlight acting out a scene, while all the other actors wait offstage for their turn. In reality, the scenes of history have played nonstop since the God of the universe spoke the world into existence - when He spoke light into the dark and shape and form into the dark void. God alone knows exactly what has happened every second of every millennium since then. He alone is aware of every thought, ever processed, in every single mind He has created. As humans, all we can do is study the writings of man to try to better understand the events of the past.

As we have learned, England had been subjected to many types of invasion by a variety of tribes and peoples. You will remember that Christianity had been brought to the original inhabitants, the Celts, of the British Isles, by a man named Patrick in the year 432. This is the man whom many call St. Patrick, and on March 17th of each year, people around the world celebrate him. Patrick was a modest man, and somehow I have a hard time believing he would approve of this adoration and title.

Off of the western coast of England, is a tiny island nation that has made a huge impact on the world. Ireland, known as the Green Isle, has

Ireland

endured a tumultuous history. As we have learned, the Celts were the first known settlers of Ireland and Britain. After the Barbarian tribes from the North came and conquered most of Britain, many of the Celts fled to Ireland. Here they lived peacefully for over five hundred years. In 795 the dreaded Vikings started their attacks, and for the next forty-five years, conquered the Celtic towns and villages, destroying monasteries as they went. By the year 840, the Vikings had settled, establishing trading ports all along the coast. Many of these trading ports, such as Dublin, Waterford, Cork, and Limerick, are still major Irish cities today. Much of the rest of Ireland remained in their traditional Irish culture and ways.

In 1014, King Brian of the most southern Irish province met the Vikings in a battle and defeated them; now he dominated the whole of Ireland as the first High King. After King Brian died, two kings fought for his much coveted position. One of these kings was Dermot MacMurrough of Leinster. King Dermot decided to ask the Normans in England to help him gain the throne.

The Earl of Pembroke, a Norman, who lived in England, saw this as a great opportunity to gain control in Ireland, so he agreed to help Dermot in exchange for his daughter's hand in marriage and the region of Leinster. This Earl of Pembroke, whose name was Richard de Claire, was also known as "Strongbow." He asked his Norman lord friends to come with him on an attack campaign in Ireland. The Norman nobles invaded Ireland, seizing land all over the country for themselves. All of this seizing and conquering made the English King, Henry II, very nervous. He considered himself the overlord of Ireland, and the Irish people, who feared a chaotic take-over of their country by the Norman Lords, supported King Henry II.

King Henry II had a large, strong army, so the Norman lords laid down their arms and submitted to the king's demands. Instead of fighting, they settled down to farm and live off of the fertile land. Soon, like the Vikings before them, the Normans adjusted and adopted the ways of the Irish. Ireland would remain under the English's control for almost two hundred years. In 1366, Lionel, the son of Edward III, and governor of Ireland, demanded that Irish-Normans stop speaking the Gaelic language and marrying the Irish people. From that point on, the Irish considered the English to be interfering, pesky foreigners.

The fourth and final Crusade...

Throughout all of these years, the Crusades were going on. As we learned earlier, these wars between "Christianity" and Islam were more like battles sporadically fought throughout the Holy Lands. The original intent was to regain control of Jerusalem. At the end of the second Crusade, Islamic invader, Saladin had control over the city. In 1198, a nobleman became

Chapter 14

Bishop Innocent III of Rome. His top priority was to destroy a Muslim army base in Egypt. Innocent III seemed to have a hard time convincing others of the importance of his mission; however, by the year 1202, he still did not have enough Crusaders or financial backing required for such an endeavor.

At this point, a group of Venetian merchants decided to become involved. They promised to provide ships for the Crusade at a much discounted price of eighty-four thousand silver coins. There was a problem, however; only about a third of the required number of Crusaders arrived in Venice on the appointed day. Also, instead of eighty-four thousand coins, there were only fifty thousand coins. An Eastern prince realized that he was in the position to bargain, so he came up with an offer. The Crusaders would receive their needed backing, if they first sailed to Constantinople and dethroned the current Eastern Empire ruler.

When Innocent III heard of this offer and the attached conditions, he forbade the Crusaders to carry out such an awful plan. By this point, the gathered Crusaders were hungry for battle, so they ignored the Pope's command. The whole plan was rotten! The Crusaders went into Constantinople and were met by the angry citizens who refused to let them leave the city.

"The Crusaders were furious. They had set out to destroy the Muslims. Now, they were stranded in Constantinople. The Crusader leaders decided to plunder Constantinople. One priest proclaimed - without the Pope's approval - 'If you rightly intend to conquer this land and bring it under Roman obedience, all who die... partake in the Pope's indulgence.' To partake in an indulgence was to be freed from enduring the earthly punishment - that is, performing the penance - for one's sins. From the perspective of many Crusaders, this proclamation provided license to do whatever they pleased in Constantinople.'"[4]

On Good Friday, 1204, crusaders, with red crosses emblazoned across the chests of their tunics, sacked the city of Constantinople. Sadly, this horrible act still impacts the world today. They ripped down and broke apart beautiful statues and pictures at the Hagia Sophia. What a terrible, terrible event in history. For sixty years after this sacking, Crusaders from the Roman church ruled the Eastern Empire. Those Eastern Empire citizens who would not live under their rule, moved southeast to Nicaea and started their own empire. There they remained until the Eastern Empire again took control of Constantinople in 1261. This was the final split of the Church. The Western church became known as the Roman Catholic Church, and the Eastern church became known as the the Eastern Orthodox Church.

Narration Break: Narrate the story of this part of Ireland's history. Talk about the fourth and final Crusade.

Genghis Kahn conquers Beijing...and everything else in his path

In this section of our chapter, we are going to travel to the East to check on the countries of the Orient. The last time we traveled over into this area, the emperor, Yangdi, had ordered the Grand Canal to be dug. After suffering under the tyranny of his son, his people rose up and rid their country of him.

To the North, in the freezing-cold, mountain country, there lived a nomadic tribe of rather barbaric people. The Mongols lived in heavy felt tents and wandered the frozen land, eating animals they killed when they stopped to sleep. These people were feared by the Chinese almost as much as the Vikings were feared throughout Europe. Like the Vikings, the Mongols conquered and destroyed everything in their paths. Mostly, the Mongols raided villages along the border. They robbed merchants and stole goods, but they did not usually venture deep into China. This all changed when a new leader named Genghis Kahn came along. Genghis was the son of a tribal chieftain of the Yakka Clan. When he became the chieftain, Genghis began working toward uniting the Mongols to attack China. He was enticed by the city of Beijing, with its beautiful houses and rich citizens. Beijing was situated south of the Great Wall, right outside of Kahn's reach.

The first step in Genghis' plan was to conquer the other Mongol tribes, so that he could be the one Mongol leader. Genghis was brutal; he attacked his fellow Mongols and demanded that they follow him or die. Soon, Genghis was the leader of all his people.

Next, Genghis and his united army of Mongols swept, like a mighty wave of destruction, down from the North, across the Chinese border. They burned and pillaged everything in their path, and they broke through the Great Wall and laid siege on Beijing. At the same time that King John of England was being forced to sign the Magna Carta, Genghis Kahn was conquering the beautiful Chinese city.

Genghis Kahn and his Mongol hordes established absolute rule wherever they went. Their empire spread, as did their terrible and fearful reputation. After capturing Beijing, Genghis turned his attention toward the west. The Muslim Empire was his next destination, and like a crazed herd of wild animals, the Mongols flew at break-neck speed to the west.

Kahn and his army struck fear into the heart of everyone they came across. The Muslim army, who was used to being considered the most terrifying force, didn't know how to handle this seemingly insane herd of Barbarians. The Mongols struck so much fear that, many times, the invaded people would lie down and give up without even a fight!

Genghis Kahn was an extremely battle-smart leader. With his well-trained, fast-moving, and completely ruthless army, he executed a series of amazing and outstanding campaigns, conquering Turkestan, Northern China, and Korea, before he moved his army to the West to take over Afghanistan, Persia, and parts of Russia.

The Mongol way of life and culture centered around fighting and strength training. Even from young ages, the boys were encouraged to develop battle skills and agility. They loved games involving horse-riding, archery, and wrestling. The Mongol Empire would continue to grow. And although the empire spread farther than any other empire up till that time, the Mongol empire would not last long. We will learn more about the rest of Genghis Kahn's family in a later chapter.

I feel the need to end our chapter on a lighter note. All of the violence of history can sometimes get to me. While I try to weave as complete a picture as possible, at times the conquering and fighting becomes too much of the picture being woven in our tapestry of history. It is at those times, I feel the need to step back and search the sea of faces crowding my view for a gentle smile, a helping hand, or a giving spirit. As I shift my focus from raiding hordes, a smile as gentle as a spring rain captures my attention.

This light in the darkness happens to belong to a man named Thomas Aquinas. Thomas started out as a son of a wealthy family. His parents wanted him to become an archbishop, but Thomas wanted to be a simple monk. After soaking himself in the church's teachings and even more of the Bible, Thomas started to preach.

Up until now, the church had separated everything from from the physical world from anything to do with the spiritual world. Thomas threw out this ridiculous idea. When he looked around him, he saw everything in the physical world as signs pointing to the Creator. You might say that Thomas Aquinas was the first Apologetics teacher!

Narration Break: Narrate the story of Genghis Kahn and Mongol hordes.

Chapter 15

Events of the Far East

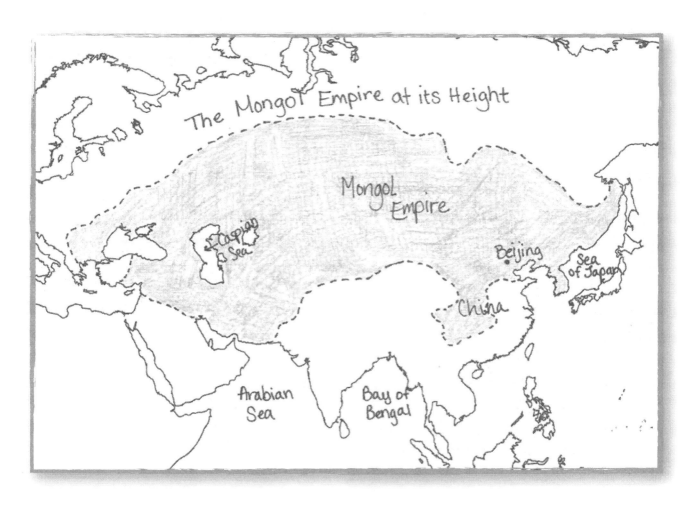

After Genghis Khan had made his terrible, sweeping rampage into China and the Middle East, his predecessors to the Mongol throne enlarged the empire. Ogodai and Monke Khan turned their eyes on Armenia, Tibet, and even more of China. Their campaigns ravaged eastern Europe, striking fear into hearts across the continent. Unfortunately, this was a violent time in the history of many European and Asian countries.

The Mongols' rule was not all bad; they were responsible for opening the Asian silk roads to the East-West merchants and travelers. By 1260, the Mongol Empire had reached the end of its expansion. The empire, which was the largest empire up to that time, stretched from the Yellow Sea in the East, all the way to the Mediterranean Sea in the West. However, this empire was not to last very long.

Genghis Khan's grandson, Kublai Khan, made himself emperor of China. He and his army already occupied the city of Beijing, but he was not satisfied with that. Kublai Khan pressed further and further south, conquering the Chinese cities and villages in their path. The Chinese fought back, using toxic gases to make deadly fogs, but the Mongols eventually over-powered them.

The Mongol Empire took land from the Byzantine Empire and the Muslim Empire; nobody seemed strong or fast enough to withstand them! After overcoming the Chinese, Kublai Khan set his gaze further to the east. He sent a message to the King of Japan, demanding that Japan surrender and lay down their weapons. The Japanese adamantly refused to surrender without a fight and scoffed at Khan's demands. The Mongols were not used to this reaction to their threats.

The enraged Kublai Khan promptly commanded that a fleet of sturdy ships be built to attack the arrogant Japanese. The Mongols sailed for the Japanese Islands, determined to beat these impudent people into submission. A strong wind commenced to blow, and soon the Mongol ships were being blown back toward China. The Mongols were stunned! They had marched through Korea and had easily conquered it, but this wind seemed almost supernatural! The superstitious Mongols decided to return to China, but many of their ships were sunk, drowning hundreds of soldiers.

Chapter 15

Seven years later, the determined Mongols tried again to attack Japan. This time, they brought many more ships and thousands more warriors. Again, they set sail for Japan. For the second time, strong winds and horrible storms (probably a hurricane) ascended on the terrified men in their ships. This storm was even stronger than the first, and its strength was so incredible that many of the Mongol ships had no hope at all of survival. Thousands of Mongol warriors were drowned and their ships capsized. Once again, the Japanese were saved from the Mongols' invasion. Kublai Khan never did conquer Japan, but even so, he ruled the largest empire on earth for over twenty years.

The travels of Marco Polo...

When I was a little girl, we played a game called "Marco Polo." This game, which is a modification of the game "tag," can be played anywhere, including a swimming pool. I always loved that game, and when I found out that Marco Polo was a real person, who lived wonderful adventures, I wanted to know all about him! Our story of this man starts back in the years of the Mongol Empire...

Marco, the son of a merchant was born in Vince, Italy. His father was away when Marco was born, and he did not return until Marco was fifteen years old. You will remember how Kublai Khan ruled the enormous Mongol Empire, from his luxurious palace in Beijing. It is interesting to note that this rather barbaric Mongol leader wanted Europeans to feel safe traveling to China. He assigned his soldiers to guard the Silk Road because he wanted merchants and visitors to feel safe and welcome as they traveled.

Chapter 15

The Silk Road was hundreds of miles long, and it passed through mountains and deserts. Water was a precious commodity, only available at the widely scattered oases. Adventurous merchants and explorers, who ventured this journey, had to be sturdy, strong, and willing to be away from home for years at a time. It took at least three years to travel to the city of Beijing from Italy.

Marco Polo's father had spent many years working for the Chinese Emperor and had come home on a mission. Kublai Khan had requested that a group of wise men come and tell him about Christianity. Marco was excited! Maybe his father, who had every intention of returning to China, would allow him to come with him. The two of them set out on what would prove to be an extremely difficult journey. Marco became ill and had to rest for long periods of time. It took Marco and his father four years for them to complete their journey.

We know about the Polos' stay in China because Marco wrote all about it in his book, _The Travels of Marco Polo_. Marco's book described, in great detail, the palace of Kublai Kahn. His words would paint a picture of the Orient for the people of Europe, so they could imagine the splendor of the Far East.

Marco stayed in China for a long time; in fact, he and his father remained for nearly twenty years. While Marco was there, Kublai Kahn made him an official in his kingdom and give him the job of settling disputes between Chinese officials. When Marco and his father finally returned home, their family members did not recognize them; they thought they had died long ago.

Narration Break: Narrate the story of this part of our story. Talk about the Kublai Kahn.

Let's stay in China a little longer; maybe we can follow the story after Marco Polo returned to Italy. Kublai Kahn, the great Mongol ruler, had promoted European visitors to China. He had his men guard the Silk Road to ensure the safety of the travelers to and from China. However, after the death of Kublai Kahn, China experienced much trouble. The emperors, who followed Kublai Kahn, were weak and unable to lead the empire successfully. The last Yuan emperor, Sun Ti, was especially bad. The people of China were tired of the Mongols and their bad rulers.

A Chinese ruler, named Zhu Yuan Zhang (ZHOO-yong-zhong), finally drove the Mongols out of Beijing and back to Mongolia. Zhu Yuan Zhang had the support of the Chinese people. He had once been a monk, a rebel bandit chief, and even a beggar on the street (during the hard reign of the previous Mongol emperor), and he had an army of followers at his disposal. It took Zhu Yuan Zhang and his army thirteen years to get the Mongols out of China.

After the Mongols were gone, Zhu Yuan Zhang established a new dynasty - the Ming ("bright") dynasty. Zhu Yuan Zhang changed his name to Hong Wu, which means "very warlike." Hong Wu moved his capital city to Nanjing, a fortified city south of Beijing, where he ruled for thirty years. Under his dictatorship, China was returned to its former glory, and the Mongols were kept at bay.

Hong Wu's grandson, Jianwen (ZHEE-on-wen), ruled after his grandfather's death, but he was overthrown by his ambitious uncle, Zhu Di (Zhoo-dee). Zhu Di changed his name to Emperor Yongle (Yong-LAY) and set about to make China even more prosperous. Under Yongle, Beijing became the capital city again. Huge renovations transform the royal palace into a "Forbidden City." This palace was as large as a city, with great, high, walls, surrounding thousands of buildings - nine thousand, nine hundred ninety-nine buidlings to be exact. This city was forbidden, because no one was allowed to see it or enter unless they were part of the royal household or servants to the royal household.

The royal family lived in this huge palace-city and enjoyed every imaginable luxury. Beautifully painted panels and silks surrounded them, while hundreds of servants waited on them hand and foot. During Yongle's rule, trade and industry flourished, and Chinese influence spread far and wide. The Ming dynasty remained in power for nearly three hundred years. Most of these years were relatively quiet and prosperous. The world became more aware of the riches of the Far East. China was also influenced by the world more, including the Muslim religion.

The Shoguns and Samurai...

While we are still in the Far East, let's take a little side trip over to Japan. You will remember our chapter about how Japan fought to become independent and culturally unique from China. We learned that a clan called the Yamato family started a dynasty, which was named after them. The emperor of Japan was not personally involved with running his country. He was more of a public figure, who lived in an elaborate palace and waved at his people during public appearances. In reality, the power belonged to the daimyos (the lords).

You see, in many ways, Japan had a feudal system very similar to England's. The king was at the top, with the daimyos (DIE-me-yo) (lords), regents (officials), and shoguns (generals) under him, and just like the European Feudal System, the Japanese had knights. European knights fought for the lord of the castle or manor; Japanese knights who were called Samurai, fought for the damyos, regents, and shoguns.

As you might guess, the samurai had to go through a long training period, just like the European knights. These fierce warriors swore their allegiance to their lord and fought furiously to protect them and to conquer anyone that the lord wanted conquered. The samurais' clothing and armor was very interesting. Much like the knights in England, the samurai wore many layers of clothing, topped by rather elaborate armor, which was painted brightly in the colors of the lord's banner.

The samurai also had a strict code of conduct like the knights. This code, called bushido, dictated that the samurai behave with great honor and bravery. Like the Code of Chivalry, bushido placed high priority on family pride. In fact, samurai practiced the rather strange habit of strutting around yelling out his name and the names of his brave samurai ancestors. Imagine how comical this would have appeared! When they actually got down to the business of fighting, the samurai were fierce indeed! They could skillfully use two swords at once, and their skill with their other weapons drove fear deep into the hearts of their adversaries.

Life of a samurai was not altogether glamorous. If they were captured by their enemy, they were expected to kill themselves in order to save face. Their religion, Zen - a branch of Buddhism - ruled the samurai's lives with strict rules for life.

Narration Break: Discuss what you learned about the Chinese and Japanese cultures and fighting styles.

HOW TO DRESS LIKE A SAMURAI

Chapter 16

The Great Civilizations of the Americas and Africa

You have probably noticed the time passing by as we study the history of the Middle Ages together. As we know, it is impossible to study everything in chronological order because many events happened simultaneously all around the world. My hope is that, as you construct your timeline, you will see how the events line up and, in many cases, overlap.

After our chapters studying the events of Europe and Asia, we are going to take a journey south of the equator and across the great Atlantic Ocean. Our first stop will be in Central America in a place which is marked "Mexico" on our current world maps. This is the land of the hot sand and blue ocean. No one knows for sure from where the Aztecs originally came, but during the Middle Ages, roaming tribes of Aztecs lived in this area. As you will no doubt remember, the Mayans lived slightly to the south of this area.

Chapter 16

The area, in which the Aztecs roamed, had other smaller tribes of nomadic "Indians," but the Aztecs were the most fierce and the largest tribe, so the Aztecs roamed about conquering the other, smaller tribes. Their behavior and way of life distinctly reminds me of the Barbarian tribes in Europe. The Aztecs, however, did not have a permanent home. They did not settle down after each conquest.

Aztec legend tells the story of how they finally found a home. It is supposed that one day the Aztecs were wandering around as usual when they came upon a huge lake with soft, muddy shores. Out in the middle of the lake was an island, and on that island, grew a huge cactus, which had an enormous eagle perched upon its branches. The Aztecs gaped in astonishment when they saw that the eagle was grasping a giant snake in its talons.

The Aztecs took this as a sign from their gods that this was to be their permanent home. The lake, Tenochtitlan (teh-NOCH-teet-lan), and the island

needed a lot of work. The Aztecs used mud and timbers to build up the island; they used logs and rocks to make pathways and roads out to their floating city. They became adept at planting gardens in floating "mat-gardens." These floating gardens were planted in soil that was loaded on grass or reed woven mats. The seeds sprouted, sending their roots down through the mat and into the water. This amazing gardening technique guaranteed the Aztecs would have produce even in a drought.

Since the Aztecs were a fighting tribe, they had to be ready for battles. They engineered their roads to be movable, so that their enemies could not reach them. The Aztecs had many enemies, and for a good reason! They were always raiding their neighbors villages to kidnap their next human sacrifice. What an absolutely terrible and depraved way to live!

We can, however, thank the Aztecs for one thing - chocolate. Yes, it was the Aztecs who discovered the delicious taste of the cacoa bean. They liked the taste so much, that they made bars from it and even drank it as a hot drink. The next time you come in from playing in the cold, to a cup of hot chocolate, you can thank the Aztecs for it!

To the south of the Aztecs, way down on the western coast of South America, was the Incan civilization. The Incas never learned to write, so there are no written records of their lives. However, we do know quite a bit about the Inca, because there are many archaeological finds in the area in which they lived. The great Incan civilization stretched about two thousand miles down the west

coast of South America. This is truly amazing! Two thousand miles is comparable to the width of our great country from the East coast to the West coast.

Because they did not keep written histories, we have to piece together what life was like for the Incas. We know by seeing the solid, well-built streets that the Incas were skilled masons. In many instances, the streets were paved with large stones, so carefully fitted together, there was no need for mortar!

We also know that merchants used llamas to transport goods along the cobbled streets.

The Incan empire stayed strong for many years. Their last, great king, Huayna Capac, divided the kingdom into two parts, which were to be ruled by his two sons after his death. As we have learned from studying history, a divided empire never stands; and this is exactly what happened to the Incas. The two brothers fought each other until both parts of the once-great empire became weak and poor. We will learn, in a later volume of history, how European explorers came into Central and South America and conquered both the Aztecs and the Incas.

Chapter 16

Narration Break: Discuss the Aztecs and the Incas.

Next, let's travel across the Atlantic Ocean from South America until we reach the great continent of Africa. What do you think of when you hear the name, "Africa"? Do you think of the hot, dry desert? Or maybe the windy savanna teeming with lions and wildebeests? Perhaps you think of Egypt with its mighty Nile River, alive with fierce crocodiles. If you thought about any of these things, you would be right! Africa is a beautiful and diverse continent, with a huge variety of ecosystems, from the most commonly thought of desert, to beautiful, lush tropical forests and mountains.

During the Ancient and Middle Ages, Africa was not well-traveled. Most visitors didn't make it any further south than the Sahara Desert. All they could see was hot sand. This is why Africa was called the "Dark Continent." Study a map of topographical Africa. As you can see, the whole central section of Africa is not desert. This area is mostly tropical forest or savanna.

The wildlife that roams these areas are amazing examples of God's creativity. African animals vary greatly from place to place. You might see monkeys and parrots - similar to those you would see in the Amazon rainforest in South America - or zebras and elephants roaming through the grasses of the savannas. You might even be fortunate enough to catch sight of a mob of meerkats, standing at attention like a small group of soldiers.

In the Middle Ages, most of Central and Eastern Africa was inhabited by tribes of nomadic people. These people didn't keep written histories and didn't build huge, durable buildings or cities. They simply lived their lives, growing food and hunting for meat to eat.

In Western and Northern Africa, however, there were well-established kingdoms. These main kingdoms of Western Africa were the empires of Ghana, Mali, and Songhai. These empires were much better known because they were more easily reached by European travelers and merchants. Europeans, who traveled here, wrote about them, leaving written histories for us to study. These civilizations were located on the western side of Africa where the continent protrudes out into the Atlantic Ocean.

Let's look a little more closely at each of these empires, starting with Ghana. Most of the people in Ghana lived in red, clay-brick houses with reed roofs. They were farming people, who also hunted and fished. The Ghanian people were known for their skill in iron working. These iron-workers could make beautiful pots and pans, copper jewelry, weapons, and tools. Ghanians may have been good farmers and excellent metal workers, but that is not how they made their fortunes. They became wealthy on gold - not *their* gold, mind you, but their neighbors' gold.

You see, the Ghanians really didn't have much gold of their own, but their neighbors to the south found tons of gold in the ground. Since the tribes with the gold had to either walk out into the Sahara Desert or go through Ghana to get north, the Ghanians took advantage of the situation. They charged a hefty "passage tax" on the gold going through their land. Since this gold was in great demand in the lands north of Ghana, they made quite a fortune on the gold, that was simply traveling through their country. Many of these gold pieces and gold jewelry were sold to merchants carrying it into places such as Egypt and other Arabian countries.

Another interesting aspect of this story is the "currency" that the southern tribes used when selling their gold. The lands to the North were rich in salt, while the southern tribes were short on it. The northern people had so much salt that they used it to buy gold. Since Ghana was in the middle, they taxed both of these commodities - gold going north and salt coming south. Ghana became extremely wealthy!

Ghana did not last forever, though. Little by little, Ghana was crumbling, succumbing to the attacks from the Muslims, who were trying to force the Ghanians to convert to Islam. As Ghana became weaker and weaker, their neighboring empire, Mali took over the salt and gold trade. Like Ghana, Mali lay between the gold in the south and the salt in the north, but Mali was not being attacked by the Muslims, because they were already an Islamic empire.

While Ghana grew weaker, Mali grew stronger, until they had become the dominant empire in Western Africa. The Mali kings were extremely powerful and controlled their peoples' lives. The most powerful of these kings, Mansa Musa, became famous throughout the Middle East when he took the Muslim pilgrimage to Mecca. Mansa Musa was the most powerful of all the Mali emperors, and after his death, the Mali empire started to lose its power and fade away.

The next empire that arose in Western Africa was the Songhai Empire. Have you ever heard the expression, "We got lost and ended up in Timbuktu"? In the Middle Ages, you could literally do this; Timbuktu was a major city in the Songhai Empire, with a population of over eighty thousand residents. This is a huge population for this time period. The people of the Songhai Empire put a lot of importance on education and culture. They built many schools - over two hundred in Timbuktu alone.

Ghana and Mali had been known for their gold and salt, but Songhai became known for its size. It grew and grew until it completely covered both of its old neighbors, Ghana and Mali. Songhai was fascinating to the visitors from the north. We know that some of these visitors were explorers who came to Africa to discover how they lived and returned to Europe to write books about it. The Songhai Empire lasted until much later, when Muslim soldiers from Morocco in North Africa came in and took control of this area.

Narration Break: Narrate the last part of our chapter.

Chapter 17

"Ashes, Ashes, We all Fall Down"
& Men of the Reformation

Parents: please pre-read this chapter!

This first part of our story is extremely sad, and I'm afraid, some of my readers will feel that it is quite scary. I think we have all learned that life during the Middle Ages was quite different than what we are used to. We have discovered many of these years were called the Dark Ages because of the lack of education, among other things. We have also learned that the people who lived during this time period had to always be aware and onguard against all types of enemies, who might be ready to attack them. From the Vikings and Muslim raiders to the Mongols and Turks, wave after conquering wave of invaders poured over the borders, pounding the land, year after year.

Nothing could have prepared Europe for what crept and lurked across the land in the year 1347. This invasion arrived as friendly trade ships docked in the bustling harbors around the Mediterranean Sea and at the busy sea-side stock yards of England and France. Onboard these sea vessels were the four-legged carriers of a deadly plague. The Black Death of Europe had arrived on the furry legs of thousands of ship-rats, and no army on earth could stamp it out. Kings and commoners would be conquered and slain by this dreaded disease.

As traders arrived from the Orient with their beautiful wares to trade, they brought stories of the terrifying sickness sweeping across the Far East. This mysterious plague left a swath of destruction so devastating and so indiscriminating that terror tolled like the peals of a funeral bell in the heart of all who heard. The Black Death, thought to have originated in the Gobi Desert, hit the Orient in the year 1328, and over a fifty-year-long outbreak left thirty-five million people dead in China. The Black Death...the words hung in the air like a threatening, menacing cloud.

As the plague rolled across Europe, the stench of death was everywhere, lingering in every street, on every corner, in every house. If a person touched the clothes of a Black Death

Did you know that the little song, "Ring Around the Rosies," came from the time of the Black Death? The ring around the rosies refers to the fever and rash caused by the plague. Ashes...we all fall down, refers to the way they burned the bodies to try to prevent the spread of the disease.
Look in your Student's Journal for the explanation for this bird outfit!

victim, they knew they would be dead within four days.

There was so much death, that soon people did not even bother to hold funerals for their loved ones. Instead, they buried the dead in mass graves and burned the clothing and belongs of the dead, in an attempt to stop the spread of the disease. Houses were left empty as whole families died.

Farms were left to decay, their crops rotting in the field. Animals roamed about the countryside, left by their dead owners to fend for themselves; many of them died of starvation or plague. London was hit by the plague in the summer of 1348, and over the next two years, twenty thousand of the city's residence succumbed to it. The plague would ravage Europe for fifty years before finally subsiding. In its wake it left two hundred million dead; a staggering one-third of Europe's population lay in the grave.

As the tide slowly turned, and the plague proceeded to fade away, a new reality set in. There were not enough survivors to meet the demand for labor. Before the plague, shops had their merchants, fields had their peasant serfs, dress shops had their seamstresses, and castles had their lords. Now, the population was two hundred million citizens smaller, leaving too few to work and supply for the needs of the survivors.

The Feudal System had always been faulty, but now it wasn't working at all. The Black Plague had become the boss; it had proven that no man-made positions could truly hold authority. So it was, the governmental system, which had been in place across the Eastern Hemisphere since the collapse of the Great Roman Empire, began to shake and fall apart. Europe was heading toward a new form of accepted government; nations arose, and as they did so, new kings united their nations and ruled their people. There were still man-made positions, assigning each citizen their place in life, but for the first time in over a millennium, the future started to brighten.

Narration Break: Discuss the Black Plague and its effects on the world.

It was during this time of change and cultural shaking that the church, too, began to feel the winds of change blowing through its pews. To understand what happened next as best as we can, we need to learn about a little thing called "indulgences."

Many hundreds of years earlier, the church came up with a plan to ensure people, who were repenting for their sins, were sincerely sorry. Church leaders felt that such repentance should be followed by a visible act to show sorrow for certain sins. This was called "performing penance." This is how they came up with indulgences were a type of certificate, which freed the owner from having to perform acts of penance. These certificates were sold on the streets by friars and priests. Citizens could literally buy the right to sin. Even though this was most likely *not* the original intent of the church officials, the church had become more and more corrupt. It seemed war, plagues, and enemy invasion ruled the earth, and the church was doing less and less to be the hands and feet of Jesus.

The state of the church was not going unnoticed by everyone! As always, God had His man for the hour, and He had His word ready to cut through the darkness. This man was a philosophy professor at Oxford University in England. John Wycliffe believed wholeheartedly that the church was not built on traditions, clergy, popes, and indulgences. He believed that the church was made up of all the people who loved Jesus and followed Him with all of their hearts and lives. He believed, and rightly so, that the church needed God's Word. They needed to have and hold their own Bible - a Bible written in their own language! Of course, this didn't go well with the church leaders of the day. They knew that if the common people could read and understand the Scriptures for themselves, the church leaders would not have as much power. God's Word is alive and active, sharper than any two-edged sword. When

we "breathe in" God's Word by reading and studying the Bible, we are more able to "exhale" holiness and Godliness. The church leaders called Wycliffe a heretic for translating the Bible, but God never allowed them to harm him or stop him from writing.

John Wycliffe died before finishing his translating project, but his work was completed by his followers. As these faithful friends handed out these new Bibles, they preached hope, forgiveness, and the power of a personal relationship with the Writer of the Scripture. A light had been turned on. No

DARK AGE could ever stand against this powerful light. GOD'S WORD is a bright light - a light that extinguishes the darkest night!

As the light of God's Word, made available in the common language, traveled across the continent, the teachings of John Wycliffe took root everywhere. Here...there! Earth's residence were beginning to know Jesus and follow Him instead of the church's teachings of man-held control. As the truth leapt and catapulted its way across borders, it fell on the ears of a Bohemian professor and priest. (Bohemia is now call the Czech Republic.) Jan Hus was a brilliant man, and when he heard the teachings of Wycliffe, he readily embraced the joyful truth.

The Bohemian church banned the teachings of Wycliffe, but Hus refused to be quiet about it. He preached the truth from the pulpit, and the church retaliated by revoking his right to preach. Hus kept right on preaching the good news of the truth. He preached that people should follow God, not the church leaders, He told them they should study the Word of God, and that if the church was not saying the same thing as the Bible, they should obey the Bible instead of the church. All of this preaching made Hus enemy number one of the church officials; the church officials turned him over to the government to be killed, because they considered his preaching to be heresy.

Jan Hus, preacher of the Gospel of Christ, was sentenced to be burned alive for preaching the truth of the Gospel. Right up to his death, Hus prayed for those binding him to the post. He blessed those who piled the wood around his feet, and he asked for forgiveness for those who set them aflame. As the wood burned closer and closer, he sang Psalms. Hus's last breaths were given to praising his Lord and Savior. As he stepped from this earth into the realms of Glory, Jan Hus left behind himself a legacy of forgiveness and grace. The lighting of that fire sent burning embers all over Europe. The truth cannot be put out! Glory!

The True Leader of the Christian church - that is, Jesus Christ Himself - had stood to His feet and called for a sifting. Soon a reform would begin deep in the very heart of all who called Him Lord. The Reformation had begun. Christianity was starting to move from being a *religion about* Christ to a *relationship with* Christ.

In our next chapter, we will hear the story of a young woman, who also lost her life at the stake. Her story is very interesting and one that has caused many theological debates since its occurrence. Did she, like Jan Hus, die for Jesus? After we read her story, take some time to think about how their stories compare. There will be a place to write about it in your Student Journal.

Narration Break: <u>Discuss the John Wycliffe and Jan Hus.</u>

Chapter 18

Interesting Events of the 1400's

Have you noticed in our story how England and France were always fighting over land? This went all the way back to the time before Richard the Lionhearted - when Vikings from England moved into Normandy, land ruled by France. When the Black Death swept through Europe, the fighting stopped for awhile. Many soldiers on both sides died from the sickness, leaving the army weaker and unable to fight about anything. When the Plague was over, the war between them started up again. All together, England and France fought and quarreled for over a hundred years. This is called the Hundred Years' War.

Henry V, one of England's most famous kings, came to the throne in 1413. He declared that he was entitled to certain land in France because his great-great-grandmother was French. She had been a princess, who had married an Englishman. Henry V, who was a rather audacious man, demanded the land "that was rightfully his" and the hand of the French Princess, Katherine, in marriage. The French king, Charles VI, absolutely refused to honor either request. The crowned prince, Charles VII, also sent along an insulting reply, which included a mocking gift.

This impertinent response, from the French royalty, angered Henry V to the extreme! He gathered his army together to attack France. Everything went badly for the English army. First, they lost several smaller battles that they should have easily won. Second, the soldiers began to get sick from the cold, damp weather. Finally, the English decided to return to their own country and try again the next year.

Chapter 18

When the French discovered the English army's plan to retreat until a later date, they sprung into action. They attacked the English at Agincourt. The Battle of Agincourt is one of the most famous in English history. The famous playwright, Shakespeare (whom we will learn about later), tells us in his play, "Henry V", that Henry gathered his cold, sick, and hungry men about him and gave them a pep talk. We don't know for sure what was said in that field, but we do know that the English defeated the French and captured a large portion of France.

Henry V took Princess Katherine to be his wife, but he never did get to be the king of France, because he died seven years later. King Charles VI also died around this time, which left both England and France without a ruler. Henry V and Katherine's one year old son, Henry VI became the king of two countries.

This marked the beginning of yet another disagreement. This time there was civil unrest between those who wanted the prince, Charles VIII (remember the one who insulted Henry V?) to become King of France and those who believed baby Henry VI would grow up to become a better ruler. Those who wanted the baby English King to rule France followed a nobleman named the Duke of Burgundy. They were called Burgundians.

All of this bickering about who should be the leader led to a cvil war in France. The English, of course, sided with the Burgundians. Charles VII, whom the French called the Dauphin (which means "prince"), knew he needed to keep control of his country's most important cities. The city of Orleans was one of these crucial cities, which the English had attacked. The Dauphin knew he had to keep the city from falling into English hands, so they desperately fought to remain in control.

It was during this siege that the Dauphin's men came to him with a young woman. Charles VII knew who she was! Everyone knew about Joan, the Maid. Charles VII had received a message from Joan saying that she had seen a vision showing her how to save the city of Orleans. The Dauphin had never met Joan before, and he wanted to test her. He gave his royal garments and crown to one of his officers and hid himself, dressed in plain clothes, in the crowd. Joan came into the room, passed by the officer in the king's clothing, and walked straight through the crowd to kneel in front of the Dauphin.

Joan proceeded to tell the Dauphin about her vision. She believed that the Saints had commanded her to gather the army and march on Orleans. After she secured that city, she was to take the Dauphin on to the Rheims Cathedral to have him crowned as King. At first, Charles VII was skeptical, but after having Joan questioned by the church officials, he decided to go with her conviction.

On they marched toward the city of Orleans, where the English and Burgundians had encamped. It was a fierce battle! Joan and her army were convinced they were fighting a holy war, with God helping. Finally, Joan and her soldiers forced the English and the Burgundians away from Orleans, thus becoming known as "Joan, the Maid of Orleans."

After Joan had escorted the Dauphin to Rheims and seen him crowned, she went on to fight battle after battle in her continued effort to free her beloved France from the grip of England. Eventually, Joan's army and Charles VII reached the final stronghold of the English and Burgundians, and here they stopped. While Charles VII bargained and communicated with the English, the army grew smaller. Soon, so many soldiers had returned home that Joan was left with a dismally shrunken army. When the English did attack, the French forces were not strong enough to withstand the pounding of the much-stronger English and Burgundians.

Much to the dismay of her followers, Joan was captured. Charles VII did not try to get Joan back. Instead, he let the English try her for witchcraft. The English and Burgundians were convinced that Joan was a witch, and they were determined to find her guilty of crimes against the church. No one was allowed to speak in her defense, so she was found guilty and condemned to be put to death. Even after this verdict was handed down, Charles VII did nothing to help this young woman, who had been so instrumental to his crowning. In the year 1431, Joan was burned at the stake for witchcraft and heresy.

After Joan's death, the French rallied themselves enough to drive the English out of their country once and for all. They gave the Burgundians a chance to swear their allegiance to France, and King Henry VI of England lost all claim to the throne of France. In his old age, Charles VII felt guilty for abandoning Joan in her time of need. He had the church re-examine the "evidence" against Joan, and twenty-five years after her death at the age of nineteen, Joan was pronounced not guilty.

Narration Break: Narrate the story of Henry V and Joan of Arc.

Remember back with me to the chapter in which we learned about the mighty Byzantine Empire. This empire had risen, strong and mighty, after Emperor Constantine had moved the capital city of the Roman empire from Rome to Constantinople. The Byzantine Empire had been attacked many times throughout the centuries. They had withstood the attacks of the Muslims from the south, the Mongols from the East, and the Russians from the North. Through all of these invasions, the great city of Constantinople had remained unconquered.

The Ottoman Turks started out as many other empires had...small and seemingly unimportant, but as time passed by, this particular band of Turks grew stronger and stronger. During the years of the Mongols' invasions, these Turks moved west, looking for a safer place to settle and picking up the Muslim way of life from those they settled nearby. Some of these people were peaceful farmers, but most of them were fierce warriors.

As the years passed, these Turks, who became known as the Ottoman Turks, wanted to expand their empire, which lay along the Byzantine border. They were determined to expand their borders and spread Islam. Through the years, the Ottoman Turks attacked cities all along the edges of the Byzantine

Chapter 18

Empire, conquering and pillaging. Soon, the Byzantine Empire was smaller than the Ottoman Empire.

After a while, all that was left of the once-great Byzantine Empire was the great, walled city of Constantinople. The city's walls kept the Turks at bay, and the people inside began to believe that their city could not be captured. According to Byzantine legend, Constantinople would remain un-captured and unconquered "until the moon went black." Of course, when anyone has this attitude, you know what is going to happen next!

One particularly strong and determined Ottoman sultan (this is what their kings were called), named Mehmed, made it his life's mission to capture the city of Constantinople. His first step was to pretend to be friends with the king of Constantinople. While he was keeping up this facade, he not only built his army up with thousands of men, he also built massively huge cannons. By the time the king of Constantinople knew what was happening, it was too late. Across the plain came monstrously huge cannons, which shot cannon balls so massive that it took many oxen to carry them.

The siege of Constantinople had raged for two months when one fateful evening, the moon became mysteriously dark. The citizens of Constantinople were terrified! They believed that their mighty city would remain unconquered until the moon went black. This surely must be a sign from God that their's was an impending doom. Both sides believed that this event, which in reality was a lunar eclipse, signaled the end of the war. The citizens of Constantinople gathered at Hagia Sophia for the last Christian service. Outside the city walls, Mehmed called for his men to give all of their remaining energy to break through the wall.

Chapter 18

On May 29, 1453, the city of Constantinople fell to the Muslim Ottoman Turks. The conquering enemy swarmed into the city like angry ants, pillaging and destroying church shrines and figurines. Sultan Mehmed had his throne placed in the center of the beautiful cathedral, the Hagia Sophia, while his men worked around him to change the once-holy building into a shrine and place of worship to their false god, Allah.

This tremendously sad event marked a very important date: the true end of the Roman empire from the ancient times. Although the effects of the Roman culture are still evident today, this was truly the first time since before the time of Christ that not one shred of the Roman world influence remained in the form of a world empire.

The story of Johannes Gutenberg and his famous printing machine...

We have learned about the early writings of the Ancient Egyptians and other ancient people groups. These types of writing were made with a sharpened stick in soft clay tablets or with paint on hard surfaces. Later, monks carefully copied the pages of the Scriptures by hand, therefore preserving the work of the ancient Jewish scribes. All of this writing took place, because humans felt the need to both leave a written history of their existence and to pass on accumulated knowledge for the coming generation. It was all painstaking work, done by hand, one piece at a time. Paper was a precious commodity and ink was scarce. During most of the Middle Ages, many people did not have access to education, resulting in mass illiteracy. As this time period drew to a close, the desire to read grew, and with it, the need for more written material.

It was during the late 1300's and early 1400's, that a man named Johannes Gutenberg lived in Mainz, Germany. Johannes was born into a wealthy family and had learned to work with metal. His uncle was a master of the mint and taught Johannes everything he needed to know.

We credit Johannes Gutenberg with the first type mold, which made printing with movable type set practical for the first time in history. This movable type setting was made with individual letters formed out of metal. These letters could be arranged to form whatever words, sentences, and paragraphs were needed. They were then locked down, stamped with ink, and run through the press, therefore stamping the whole of the writing onto large pieces of paper.

Johannes and his workers were able to print out beautiful books on his printing press. The most important books Gutenberg printed on his press were Bibles for the common people of Europe. You can see a replica of Gutenberg's printing press on display in his original workshop in Mainz, Germany.

Narration Break: Talk about the fall of Constantinople and Gutenberg's printing press.

Chapter 19

Kings of the Day

In our last chapter, we learned about how France and England fought over land in France. We learned that King Henry V, the famous king of England married the French princess, Katherine, and had a little boy, whom they named with the not-so-terribly-creative name, Henry VI. After both Henry V of England and the little boy's maternal grandpa, King Charles VI of France both died, one year old Henry VI became king of both England and France. After a power struggle between the two countries, the English were forced out of France.

As Henry VI became a man, he was a good king, much better than his father before him. He was a deep thinker, and he liked to read and contemplate the writings of the church and ancient philosophers. He spent hours quietly reading his books. As he learned from his reading, Henry VI tried to be kind and fair to everyone, even refusing to kill his enemies. Years went by, and as Henry VI grew older, his mind became weaker. He experienced spells of insanity more and more often. As his mind weakened, it became evident that he needed someone to help him rule, at least until he was stronger.

After much debate, Henry's court officials came to the conclusion that England needed a substitute ruler, someone who could help when needed, but would also be willing to step down when Henry was feeling better. The man for the job seemed to be a distant cousin, the Duke of York. As you can probably guess, this duke enjoyed being king. When the time came to step down, and return the throne to Henry, the duke refused. Somehow this does not surprise me at all!

This disagreement quickly escalated into a civil war, as the king and his supporters, and the duke and his supporters fought over the crown of England. This war became known as the War of the Roses, because both parties involved had a rose on their family crest. One rose was white, and the other was red.

The duke was killed in battle, and it seemed that Henry VI's reign would continue uninterrupted, but the duke's son stepped in to take his father's place against the king. This son of the Duke of York was a strapping young man of nineteen years of age His name was Edward, and he was determined to be the king of England. Edward gathered his army and those loyal to his cause, and the War of the Roses continued, as Edward's army attacked the Royal forces. This time the Yorks were victorious, and Edward had Henry VI removed from the throne and clapped into prison.

Edward took the throne, and he proved to be a good king. He worked hard at pleasing his people. Edward might have remained in favor except he had one, small problem - he had secretly married the wrong woman. This woman, name Elizabeth Woodville, was older than Edward, and she had been married before. Edward kept his marriage to Elizabeth a secret because he knew his family would not appreciate the fact that her first husband had died fighting for Henry VI! Only when his family tried to arrange a wedding for

Chapter 19

Edward with a foreign princess did he come out with the truth about his marriage to Elizabeth.

When the news of the king's marriage came out, Edward decided to move his wife and her family to the palace. He gave Elizabeth's brothers important positions in his government. The people of England did not like the fact that Edward had kept his marriage a secret or that he had given so many important government positions to his brothers-in-law.

When Edward heard that the people were coming to remove him from the throne, he ran away. King Henry VI was returned to his place on the throne, and the people rejoiced to have their king back. However, Edward was not gone for good! He was busy gathering an army to help him get re-crowned. He marched back into England and captured King Henry VI again. No one knows for sure, but many believe that Edward arranged to have the elderly king murdered in prison. Once again Edward was on the throne. He ruled for twelve years before he died and left the throne to his twelve year old son, Edward V.

Being only twelve years old, Edward V was too young to rule England on his own; therefore, his father's brother, Richard, offered to help him rule until he was old enough to do so on his own. Richard took over the throne and named himself King Richard III of England. Poor Edward V and his younger brother soon mysteriously disappeared. Rumor said that both youngsters were locked away to starve to death in the Tower of London. No one ever discovered the truth about their disappearance, but everyone has always been quite sure that their Uncle Richard had something to do with their demise.

King Richard III was not destined to keep the throne, which he had so cruelly secured for himself. A mere two years after he became king, another distant, but royal cousin, Henry Tudor, laid claim to the English throne. In 1485, the two of them met with their armies at a battleground named Bosworth Field.

Richard's army, nearly twice the size of Henry's, lost that day, and Richard was killed. Henry Tudor became the next king that day and thus ended the War of the Roses. The Tudor age of England had begun.

Narration Break: <u>Discuss the War of the Roses.</u>

During this time, in not-so-far-away Russia, lived a mighty ruler named Ivan the Great. Russia had been settled first by the Slavs and then by the Vikings, who had come and settled down there. This new, mingled people spread out over a vast area of Russia.

When the Vikings had first come, it was a Viking warrior, named Rurik, who first settled there, and the Slavs called him and his people the "Rus." This is how we get the word "Russians." As generations passed, the Slavs and the Vikings descendants grew into tribes, which scattered all over the land. Just like India, China, Japan, and Korea, Russia was divided up into clans and tribes, which were not united under one king.

Through the years, the Rus chieftains grew stronger, but they were not united, which made them unable to conquer many of their enemies. Finally, one Russian prince, who was strong enough to unite the cities and tribes in one nation, came to the throne of his clan. Ivan was a prince of Moscow, and he was tired of how the chieftains and princes were always fighting amongst themselves. Ivan believed that all of this division made them weaker and more susceptible to enemy invasion. He was right, too! Already the Mongols, who had swept through the continent years before, had a hold on important cities, including Moscow.

Ivan was a descendant of the mighty Viking, Rurik, and was determined to be the one to shake off the control of the Mongols and unite his people. After he had formed a large enough army to rid his city and province of the Mongols living there, he set out to conquer the other cities and provinces. Ivan became known as "Ivan the Great," because he united Russia.

As Ivan built up Moscow, he had an important government center built right in the center of the city. This government center is called the Kremlin, and it is still used today. You might have seen pictures of the great onion-domed cathedral, which is part of Ivan's building project in Moscow.

Ivan the Great was a good king, who cared for his country a great deal. He worked hard to advance education and culture in Russia. By the end of Ivan's reign, Moscow had become the center of the Eastern Orthodox Church, because Constantinople and the Hagia Sophia had fallen to the Muslim Ottoman Turks. Ivan the Great became known as the first Czar of Russia.

Ivan's grandson, also named Ivan, was not like his grandfather in any other way. The second Ivan became known as Ivan the Terrible. He was so terrible, in fact, that he was afraid his enemies - this group was comprised of everyone besides himself - were plotting against him. Even Ivan's advisors were under constant scrutiny. Many of them lost their lives because of Ivan's paranoia. Ivan's secret police were known for being corrupt and greedy. In their King's name, they broke in and stole from the wealthier citizens.

After his beloved wife died, Ivan the Terrible went rather insane. His hair fell out, and he became even more worried that someone was trying to take his throne. During an argument with his son, who was a grown man and heir to the throne, Ivan hit him on the head and killed him. For the rest of his life, Ivan wore black and refused to be comforted. His death brought the end of the Rurik Dynasty.

Now we are going to step back a few years in time and travel to the southwest of where we have have been in Russia. Our next stop in our story takes place in a small country, which runs along the west coast of Spain. Portugal may be small in size, but it holds an important place in history. In our next chapter, we will learn about the famous Spanish king and queen, whose names you may have heard. King Ferdinand and Queen Isabella of Spain are often mentioned when we read stories of Christopher Columbus, the explorer credited for discovering America.

Chapter 19

In this chapter, however, we will learn about a famous Prince of Portugal. Henry was the fourth son of the Portuguese king, so he grew up knowing that in all probability, he would never have the throne. This did not bother Henry, however, because he had other interests. Henry loved the sea.

Portugal has a very long coastline because its entire western border lies on the Atlantic Ocean. This country is known for its numerous picturesque bays and harbors, where many ships and sailboats bob in the blue water.

Prince Henry of Portugal invested his wealth to train the Portuguese sailors, to make them into expert navigators. People started calling him Henry the Navigator because of all the time, money, and interest he invested in the sailing men of his country. So what caused Henry to become so interested in building his country's navigation system? Well, when Henry was younger, he

spent some time in the army. It was while he was in Northern Africa fighting the Muslim Raiders, who had taken control of an important port city, Henry came to an important conclusion. He realized that if Portugal wanted to trade directly with the spice merchants of Western Africa, they needed to be able to sail better. This is when Henry decided to invest his life and wealth into the Portuguese navigation system.

When he returned home to Portugal, Henry paid mapmakers (cartographers) to make new and better maps. He paid for a new School of Navigation, and he ordered better ships made. These new ships were lighter and faster. They were also more easily handled in rough waters. Portuguese sailors were taught how to use new sailing devices, such as the compass. They also were taught how to sail using the stars as their guides, a different star for every season. All of these improvements made the Portuguese some of the best sailors in the world. In fact, we still use their system of knots for measuring nautical speed.

After Henry had equipped his sailors with fine tools of the trade and trained them how to sail better, he invested in expeditions to go south down the coast of West Africa. Unfortunately, Henry had a new problem. Most people were afraid to travel down into what they called "The Sea of Darkness." Sailors of that day were convinced that as they went further South, the sun would get so hot, the water would boil, cooking them on their ships.

Finally, in 1434, Henry found someone who was

brave enough to face the certain peril of the Sea of Darkness. What this brave sailor found was water conditions no different than those along the Portuguese coastline. After this discovery was made, other sailors decided they were brave enough to try it too.

Henry had fond hopes of his ships finding their way all the way around the southern tip of Africa and up the other side to India. This did not happen during Henry's lifetime, however. The maps of the Middle Ages did not show how truly HUGE the continent of Africa is. Henry the Navigator had helped Portugal becoming a leader in navigation, contributed to the growth of trade with Africa, and dispelled the myths of the Sea of Darkness, but he did not reach India. It would be much later that an explorer would come along and discover how truly immense Africa is.

Narration Break: Discuss Ivan the Great and Henry the Navigator.

Chapter 20

Ferdinand & Isabella

In our last chapter, we spent time with Henry the Navigator, the Prince of Portugal, who helped his country's navigation and expanded the trade route with Western Africa. In this chapter of our story, we will meet a famous king and queen, who ruled in Spain together during the mid to late 1400s.

If you have heard the story of Christopher Columbus, you will no doubt recognize their names. (We will spend much more time focusing on the life and explorations of Christopher Columbus in our next volume of history.)

Many years before the rule of Ferdinand and Isabella, Islamic raiders had

conquered most of Spain. The Christians, who still lived in Spain united themselves to fight against the Muslim Kingdoms. These battles were carried out by small Christian kingdoms all over Spain. After the Muslims were pushed out of Spain, the Christian kingdoms joined together to form three larger kingdoms: Aragon, Castile, and Portugal.

King Enrique, of the kingdom of Castile, had big plans to make his kingdom the most powerful in Spain.

His plans included arranging a marriage between a rich nobleman and Enrique's own thirteen year old sister, Isabella. In return, the nobleman was to provide Enrique with enough soldiers to fight and conquer the other kingdoms.

Isabella was horrified! The nobleman was much older than she, and the thought of the marriage made her want to hide. She prayed for deliverance from this terrible fate. On his way to the wedding, the nobleman became ill and died. Thus, Enrique's plan failed, and Isabella was free.

Four years later, Enrique again tried to use his sister to further his political gain. This time he promised her hand in marriage to the much older king of Portugal. Seventeen year old Isabella was again desperate to escape this fate. Secretly, she wrote a letter to the Prince of Aragon, asking him to consider marrying her and joining their countries. Isabella did not know Prince Ferdinand of Aragon, but she had heard that he was handsome, honorable, and best of all, close to her own age. When she received word that Ferdinand would meet her in secret, Isabella ran away in the middle of the night to the place they had agreed upon. After discussing their situation, the young people decided to be married immediately.

Although their marriage enraged King Enrique, what could he do about it? His sister was already married, so he had to break off his plans with the king of Portugal. When King Enrique died six years later, Isabella became queen of Castile. Four years after she took the throne of Castile, Isabella watched her husband, Ferdinand, become King of Aragon. Together, they united their countries, making one large kingdom of Spain.

Isabella and Ferdinand declared Spain to be a Christian kingdom and made any other religion illegal. They turned their attention to the one remaining area of Spain still under Muslim rule. The small, mountain kingdom, Granada, fought for ten, long years against Ferdinand and Isabella's armies before finally falling under their control, making Spain a united and completely "Christian nation."

For the most part, Ferdinand and Isabella are considered to be some of the best rulers of Spain. There are, however, a few sad events that happened during their reign. Because the king and queen had declared Spain to be a

Christian kingdom, outlawing all other religions, all of the Jews, who lived in Spain, had to leave. This was a very sad event in Spanish history.

Narration Break: Discuss the story of Ferdinand and Isabella.

India ruled by the Mughals...

In the Middle Ages, spices were extremely important. There were no refrigerators or freezers to keep meat fresh. Spices were used to make meat taste better even when it was almost spoiled. Because of this, spices were almost literally worth their weight in gold. Kingdoms that could grow such spices became rich. (Remember the salt trade in Africa?) India was also a land rich in spices.

You will remember that a strong leader, Chandragupta, had united much of the northern part of India. Under the reign of the Gupta Dynasty, India remained united, strong, and peaceful. This was the Golden Age of India. Then the Huns came. India was able to fight them off, but all the wars weakened their once-strong kingdom. Eventually, the Indian Empire crumbled apart, separating into smaller, weaker kingdoms. After the Huns' invasions, India's kingdoms were constantly fighting amongst themselves. They were not able to work together to ward off other invaders, and eventually a strong Muslim warrior came and conquered one of India's largest kingdoms, Delhi. This unnamed warrior declared himself to be the Sultan of Delhi.

During this time, India also suffered from floods some years, famines the next, and diseases that wiped out whole villages at a time. India became more and more poverty-stricken. Finally, a strong leader, who was capable of uniting India, came along. this leader was an Ottoman Turk named Babur.

Babur was a descendant of Genghis Kahn. With his strong army of fast and furious warriors, Babur attacked the kingdom of Delhi. The sultan of Delhi was not concerned, however. After all, his army outnumbered Babur's army more than eight thousand to one!

Babur had something that the sultan did not have, though - horses and muskets. The sultan had war elephants, which were commonly used at this time, and his soldiers were armed with spears, bows, and swords. The soldiers on horses could easily dart between the legs of the ponderous elephants, allowing Babur's soldiers to attack and shoot from behind or whatever side they chose.

In the end, Babur and his army won the battle; Babur conquered Delhi and named himself the new sultan. The surrounding kingdoms quaked in fear because they knew they were next. They were afraid that the Muslim Babur

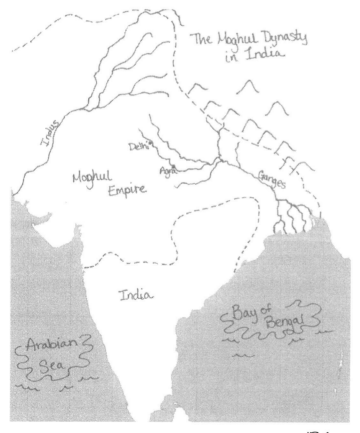

would attack and loot their Hindu temples. However, Babur was not interested in forcing India to be a Muslim country. Instead, he encouraged cultural development and education. Babur wanted India to become the nation with the best culture in the world. The new sultan ruled his new kingdom only four years, but his descendants ruled for years to come. They were called the

Chapter 20

Mughal Dynasty, because Babur was a descendant of Genghis Kahn the Mongol.

Sometimes when I am writing the accounts of history, it is easy for me to start thinking about all of the information that I am "supposed" to convey to my readers in order for them to have a complete picture of history. We, as students of history, need to remember to stay focused on the people of history, not only on the events. It is the people who created history, and unless we know them at least at some level, we will truly not know history. As I have been writing the account of how the Muslims invaded and overthrew civilization after civilization, I have found myself yearning to see it from an individual's eyes. How did it feel to be living in Constantinople when the Ottoman Turks broke through the city wall? How did it feel to be a Christian monk watching the beautiful Hagia Sophia - the Church of Holy Wisdom - being turned into a place of pagan worship? How did it feel to be one of the hundreds of Christian Eastern Orthodox scholars who were forced to run for their lives?

These heroes of the faith not only fled for their own lives, but also rescued many of the church's prized possessions, the ancient Greek manuscripts. Although the ancient authors had been all but forgotten for hundreds of years, these scholars, of the Biblical scrolls of old, risked their lives to save them for future generations. As they fled to the west, these scholars searched for a place to re-establish their places of study, and as they did, a new interest began to arise - an interest in learning and in the ancient writings. These writings were not only Biblical transcripts but also writings from Ancient Greek philosophers.

This interest was a rebirth - or as it is now called, a Renaissance, of interest in Ancient Greek art, rhetoric, and writing. The Renaissance scholars were similar to the ancient writers; they stressed practical human actions. These new scholars focused on the original intent and language of the Scriptural text. Their motto became "Back to the sources!" This is when Johannes Gutenberg became involved, printing Bibles in "the language of the people."

Another man, Desideruis Erasmus, became an important part of this awakening. Erasmus was a monk who became increasingly disenchanted with the corruption, which ran rampant in the church. Erasmus, like Gutenberg, believed that if people could have the Word of God in their hands, written in a language they could understand, the TRUTH would set them free. Reform would come to the church, and the people of God would be united and changed.

In 1516, Erasmus wrote and published a New Testament. This Greek translation was called the *Textus Receptus*, or the Received Text, and it allowed people to read the holy Word in its original translation. A spark had been ignited!

Narration Break: Discuss the last part of our chapter.

Chapter 21

A "Hot Headed" Monk Spins the World on its Ear

We have learned that it is impossible to separate the history of the Christian church from the history of the world, and in this chapter, we will see how one man of the church spun the whole world on its ear. By this point in history, the Dark Ages had come to an end, and the Renaissance - a new way of thinking - was swelling onto the world scene. A few chapters ago, we learned about an issue in the church caused by the selling of indulgences. Do you remember what indulgences were and how they came about? Just as a short review… The Roman Catholic church taught that if a person was truly repentant of their sin, they should show it by doing acts of penance. Indulgences were certificates that exempted the owner from having to do penance. The selling of these certificates became a lucrative business for friars and priests all over Europe. Along with selling of indulgences came the moral decline of the church and the culture in general.

With the dawning of the Renaissance, increasing numbers of people began to question the practice of indulgences. Call for reform had started bubbling under the surface. This is where our story picks up. We will step into the year 1505 and meet up with a German lawyer, who just happens to be ambling by in our storyline…

In the year 1505, Martin Luther was beginning a life journey. On this particular day, Martin was almost hit by lightning, so his nerves were just a wee bit rattled! You'll have to excuse the terrified expression on his usually dignified and somewhat placid face. You see, Martin was so terrified by the near lightning strike that he cried out to God to save him, and in the heat of the moment (quite literally!), he promised that he would become a monk if his life was spared. God did save Martin and didn't allow the lightening bolt to strike him directly. Martin, being a man of his word, worked at becoming a monk. There was a problem, however. The more Martin studied, the more he was struck by the depravity of his sin and the stark contrast made by the Holiness of God. The terror of God's wrath against him (probably reminiscent of the sizzling lightning bolt) drove him to spend hours in confession.

Poor Martin was so driven by guilt and anguish that his monastery sent him away to study at the University of Wittenberg. After a while, Martin became the Bible professor at Wittenberg, but still, he was haunted by this one question: How can anyone please a righteous God? As Martin searched the Bible for the truth, he was led to read Romans 1:17.

"For therein is the righteousness of God revealed from faith to faith: as it is written, The just shall live by faith."

Finally! Martin had an answer! Righteousness was not only a condition but an act of God. God declares those who come to repentance, through Jesus' death and resurrection, righteous. Grace and mercy, through the forgiveness of sin, by the blood of Jesus shed on the cross, brought former sinners to righteousness. Martin's spiritual eyes were opened, and as the Scripture says, the truth set him free!

Martin's excitement, over finding what the Bible says about forgiveness and righteousness, set him on fire for the truth.

"The righteousness of God is that righteousness by which through grace and mercy God justifies us by faith. I felt myself reborn! ... The passage of Paul became my gate to heaven... works do not make one righteous. Righteousness creates good works." Martin Luther

As is usually the case when God enlightens the mind and heart of someone who seeks Him, Martin's great transformation annoyed many who liked things just the way they were. The selling of indulgences was a long-running tradition that made a lot of money for many high-ranking church officials. Greed and selfishness fueled many abuses against the common man. Instead of being the hands and feet of Jesus, these indulgence salesmen were giving Jesus a bad name. Martin detested this practice and was appalled to see a monk selling his wares on the streets of his town.

Martin had been appointed to be the pastor of a village near the German region of Mainz, the area in which Johannes Gutenberg lived. As Martin Luther walked the streets of his village, he scowled whenever he saw the monk, Tetzel, selling indulgences to the people. Tetzel would sing out, "As soon as the coin in the coffer rings, the soul from purgatory springs!"

Martin's blood boiled until finally, he could stand it no longer. In October of 1517, Martin scribbled a list of ninety-five topics, which he wished to debate Tetzel on, and nailed them to the door of the church. Little did he know what his Ninety-five Thesis would do to the world.

The Pope declared Martin Luther to be a "drunk German" but three years later, when Martin was still speaking out about his convictions, the pope published a bull (a statement written in the pope's name) entitled "Arise, O Lord." In his bull, the pope called Luther a "wild pig," who had invaded the Lord's vineyard, the church. Luther threw his copy of the pope's bull in a bonfire.

Two months after Luther's bonfire, he received a letter from the Holy Roman Emperor himself. The letter told Martin to come under the protection of the Emperor and answer in regard to his books. We call this meeting the "Diet of Worms." No, Martin was not made to eat worms because of his books. "Diet" is the Latin word for an imperial meeting, and the meeting took place in the German city of Worms. Thus, the Diet of Worms.

Martin fully expected to lose his life at this meeting. There had been others, who had been to come "under the protection of the Holy Roman Emperor" to a diet, and had never been seen again. As he stood there, with sweat glistening on his brow, Martin was filled with conviction of the truth he had learned. When questioned if he defended what he had written Luther responded, "My conscience is captive to the Word of God. I cannot and I will

not recant anything, for to go against conscience is neither right nor safe.
God, help me." God safe-guarded Martin's life that day.

A few years, after the Diet of Worms, Luther married a young lady, who
had been a nun. Twenty-six year old Katherine von Bora was a feisty, red-
head. She and Martin went on to have six biological and four adopted
children; life was good for the Luther family.

Narration Break: Discuss the story of Martin Luther.

As Martin Luther was defending his Ninety-five Thesis, another group of
people was starting their pilgrimage from the darkness of erroneous teachings.
The citizens of Zurich, Switzerland, were standing up together, under the
guidance of their priest, Ulrich Zwingli. As these two men, Luther and Zwingli,
both worked for reform in the church, their followers worked to unite them.

The meeting was planned to happen in the German city of Marburg. The
two men agreed to meet and discuss uniting; they concluded that only one
important issue divided them - transubstantiation. This is a long word which
has to do with taking the Lord's Supper. Luther did not agree with the Roman
Catholic or Eastern Orthodox Churches about how Christ is present at
communion services. These two churches believe that the wine and bread
physically became the body and blood of Christ. Martin Luther did not believe
these elements changed, but he did believe that "Christ's body is present with
the visible elements." [5] This became known as consubstantiation. Zwingli, on
the other hand, held the belief that Jesus' words, "This is my body," simply
meant, "This symbolizes my body." All of this may or may not have much

significance to us, but to these two church reformers, it was enough to keep them from uniting.

When Lutheranism was outlawed by Catholic leaders, a group of Lutherans protested so loudly, they were called "Protestants." This name was soon being used to describe both Lutheran and Reform church. But who was the Reform Church?

Our next reformer is well-known as the father of the Reformed Church. John Clavin started his journey as a Renaissance leader. He was one of the men who encouraged people to think for themselves concerning the Bible and what God said through the Scriptures. In our time, when we hear the name "humanist," we think of someone who worships human thinking, completely excluding God from the picture, but during the Renaissance, a humanist was someone who emphasized personal, human involvement with their relationship with God.

Renaissance humanists believed God was interested in speaking to the individual humans He had created. John Calvin was a Renaissance humanist. He gave speeches, liberally sprinkled with quotes from Luther and Erasmus.

Chapter 21

What John Calvin said rattled the government of Calvin's homeland, France, and he was forced to flee for his life to Switzerland. Soon after leaving the University of Paris, Calvin dedicated himself to being a Christian and Protestant. He wrote the first systematic summary of Protestant theology, a book called "Institutes of the Christian Religion." Calvin's message met with acceptance in some circles and resistance in others, but he would go on to become considered one of the leading reformists of the church.

As reformer after reformer came on the scene, the school of thought became that a government had a right, and indeed the responsibility, to enforce the chosen theological views. In Zurich, Switzerland, a group of believers first decided to question several practices enforced by the church and government.

All through the Middle Ages, there had been a darkness over the cultures and peoples of the earth. The collapse of the Roman Empire, the invasions of the Huns, Vikings, and Mongols, followed by the Black Death, all spread fear deep into the hearts of the citizens of Earth. As we know, the only One, who can spread true light and hope, is the One who died to take the sins of the world. As the Renaissance slowly awakened Europe, God used many people to question long-held beliefs that had held His people captive for many centuries. Martin Luther, the father of the Lutheran

Menno Simons

Church, John Calvin, the father of the Reformed Church, Felix Manz, the Father of the Anabaptists, and Menno Simons, father of the Mennonites... the list goes on and on.

In today's world, the Christian Church is divided by denominations, each holding to their own theology. However, it is interesting to note that the founders of these very denominations were, at the beginning, united in their cause, and that was to bring hope and Jesus to the common man.

Narration Break: Discuss the last part of our chapter.

Chapter 22

The Strange & Disturbing Life of Henry VIII

In our last chapter, we learned about some of the most important leaders of the Reformation. The world was changing, and those who were willing to change along with it were coming out of the shadows of the Dark Ages. As is usually the case when change happens, there were those who fought against it or, even worse, tried to use the new way of thinking to their own selfish advantage. Thus is the story of Henry VIII.

This story is rather unusual and will take some extreme concentration to keep straight in your mind. First, remember back to when we learned about the War of the Roses. Richard, King Edward V's brother, took the throne away from twelve year old King Edward VI of England. Edward and his younger brother disappeared without a trace, and Richard crowned himself as Richard III of England. His reign didn't last long, however, when a distant cousin laid claim to the throne. Henry Tudor ushered in the Tudor age of England, and crowned himself Henry VII.

King Henry VII was concerned about his royal heirs. He wanted to ensure that his son would become king, followed by his grandson, and so on. In order to make sure his son would become king, Henry VII orchestrated a wedding between his son and the princess of Spain. This probably doesn't seem like that big of a deal, but what if I told you that the groom, Prince Arthur, was two years old, and his bride, Catherine, was only three? These two weren't actually legally married, but this wedding ceremony, which is called a proxy, (because adults had to stand in for the toddlers), ensured that these two HAD to get married just as soon as they possibly could.

When Arthur and Catherine were fifteen and sixteen years old, they got married again; this time, they stood up for themselves. Unfortunately, Arthur died not long after their wedding, leaving Henry VII to pass the the crown to his next oldest son, Harry.

This left Henry VII in a predicament, indeed! He wanted his son, Harry to marry Catherine, Arthur's young widow. They needed to have a son to keep the crown and throne in the family. This was an unusual situation, so King Henry VII went to the pope for help - he needed special permission for Harry and Catherine to marry. The pope gave his approval and the wedding took place.

When Henry VII died two months later, Harry was placed on the throne, and his name was changed to Henry VIII. Years passed by, and Catherine and Henry VIII did not have a son. Instead, they had a daughter, whom they named Mary. Henry VIII was becoming desperate! His wife, Catherine, was getting too old to have children. What could he do? He decided that the only thing he could do was to get rid of Catherine. But how? They had been married for more than eighteen years!

Finally, when Henry VIII was about to give up, he heard something that gave him hope. It was at this time that Martin Luther was speaking out about the pope being wrong about indulgences. When he heard this, Henry VIII reasoned that if the pope was wrong about indulgences, then he could be wrong about other matters, too... matters like his marriage to Catherine! After all, it was the pope who had been the authority behind his marriage eighteen years earlier.

The pope was very angry, and he adamantly refused to annul Henry and Catherine's marriage. The pope's response infuriated Henry! He was so angry that he declared all of England's Christians free of the pope's authority. Henry VIII made himself the Supreme Head of the Church in England. He decided he didn't need approval from the pope to divorce Catherine. Her inability to produce a son gave him the right to be rid of her, so Henry sent her away and married a young woman from his court.

Anne Boleyn became wife number two. Henry was ecstatic to find that he was going to be a daddy again. Finally! He would have his son, but he didn't. A little girl, Elizabeth, was born to Anne and Henry. Henry was so angry, he ordered Anne to be beheaded. (I wonder how he would take the news that it is the father who determines the gender of the baby!) Henry married wife number three within two weeks of the unfortunate end of wife number two.

Wife number three was a lady named Jane Seymour. As providence would have it, Jane gave Henry the son, whom he so desperately wanted. Sadly, Jane herself died soon after the baby was born. Henry did not spend much time grieving for Jane. Instead, he ordered artists to go all over Europe and paint portraits of all the beautiful princess. He was shopping for wife number four, who would hopefully be the mother of his second son. When the portraits were all finished and brought before the selfish king, he settled on a woman named Anne of Cleves, a German princess, whom he deemed beautiful enough to be his wife number four.

When Anne of Cleves arrived for the wedding, Henry was rather startled; it seems the portrait artist's depiction did not quite capture the princess' true appearance. King Henry VIII did not want to anger the lady's family, so he went through with the marriage. Afterward, however, he decided that he could not live with her, and because he was the Supreme Head of the Church in England, he declared his marriage annulled. With that, wife number four gladly ran out the door! After all, the man, whom she had come to marry, was a far cry from the handsome king she had imagined!

Henry was on the look out for wife number five. It did not take him long to find her. Catherine Howard was around only a little while before the self-centered king had her beheaded. There doesn't appear to be any reason for her death; maybe the king was just bored.

Wife number six, Catherine Parr, was a nurse, and if I may say, she was very brave! By this time, Henry VIII was old and ill, and Catherine took care of him until the end of his life. She was also a good mother to his three children.

Henry VIII died, leaving the Tudor line to his well-beloved son, Edward VI. Edward was a little boy when his father died, so his uncle helped him rule. Little King Edward VI was a sickly child; he wasn't very strong or big, and he had a bad cough that wouldn't go away. As he got older, Edward did not get better. Instead, he was bedridden by the time he was fifteen years old. Eventually, the son of Henry VIII died, leaving the throne to his sisters, Mary and Elizabeth. We will learn about the daughters of Henry VIII in our next chapter; theirs' is a story that changed the course of history.

Narration Break: Discuss the last part of our chapter.

Next, we are going to look at the story of a man, who wanted everyone in England to have a Bible that they could read. William Tyndale had studied Greek and Renaissance humanism at Cambridge University in England, and he had become obsessed with interpreting the New Testament into English. There was only one problem, though; Tyndale's bishop would not give his permission for the project.

Church leaders did not want private parties to translate the Scriptures. They believed that this job should be done by an authorized group of scholars, who could combine their knowledge. They feared that any single translator could easily pass their own personal opinion and prejudices into the translation.

William Tyndale, however, believed that God would guide his efforts in the translating process. When he realized the bishop was going to try to stop him from translating the New Testament into English, Tyndale ran away to Germany to complete the publishing process. In the year 1526, a printer in Worms, Germany, published and printed six thousand copies of Tyndale's New Testament. When the New Testaments poured into England three months later, English bishops bought thousands of them. Why would they do this? Had they unexplainably and unexpectedly become extremely interested in Tyndale's English translations? Hardly!

The bishops bought the Tyndale New Testaments to fuel a huge bonfire. They were so determined to keep this "inferior" translation out of the common man's hands that they bought and burned literally thousands of these Testaments. The Bible bonfires failed to stop William Tyndale. He simply used the money to update his New Testament. The bishops' purchases paid for the revised Testaments, which ran off of the printing presses by the thousands.

Soon, there were updated Tyndale New Testaments being smuggled into

England in flour sacks. Eventually, the common people of England would hold in their hands the Word of God, the Story of their Savior and Lord, written in their own language. It wasn't going to be the New Testaments in the English flour sacks that would eventually spell big trouble for William Tyndale, however.

Do you remember how Henry VIII decided to get rid of his first wife, Catherine? William Tyndale heard about this and decided to speak out about it. In 1530, he published a tract denouncing King Henry's behavior. William Tyndale was arrested and killed for speaking out against the King. As he died, he prayed these words, "Lord! Open the king of England's eyes!"

The Scriptures promise us that God causes all things to work together for the good of those who trust Him. William Tyndale trusted God, and God used the very person who had caused Tyndale's demise to finish the work William started with translation. In 1538, King Henry VIII authorized and approved the Matthew's Bible, a completed edition of Tyndale's work. The following year, King Henry had a copy of this Bible placed in every English church.

It was likely because of the rift between Henry VIII and the church officials that the king authorized this project; he knew that the church officials were not in favor of it. King Henry VIII, as we know, was not a godly or even a good man, but God can do anything He wants, and He honors those who serve Him, sometimes causing even ungodly people to do things that bring Him glory.

Narration Break: Narrate the story of William Tyndale.

Chapter 23

The Reformation & Counter Reformation
and Two Tudor Queens

As we have traveled together through the last few chapters of our story, we have seen the Roman Catholic Church starting to lose her grip on the world. A wave of reform had begun to build. Looking back, we can see that wave crash on the shore of world history as Martin Luther, the German lawyer-turned-monk, with an obsession for the truth, pounded a nail into the heavy wooden door of his church. As the parchment fluttered in the breeze and the words written there were whispered from ear to ear, the idea of reform grew in the hearts of people all across Europe.

For centuries, the Roman Catholic Church had told people what to believe and what was right and wrong. To say that the entire church was corrupt is not true, but just as in every situation, there were those with pure intentions and motives, and there were those who were driven by greed and other wrong motives. The church needed a sifting.

Martin Luther's writings garnered the attention of many. Reform was eminent. We have learned about the group who became known as the Protestants, but there were also those inside the Catholic Church, who wanted reform and change. These Catholic reformers, had wanted change even before Martin Luther's Ninety-five Theses were nailed to the church door. Their plans for reform had to be rethought, however, when the Protestants came along.

At first, the Catholic reformers wanted to reunite with the Protestant reformers who had left the church. A split in the church was the last thing they wanted to happen. Remember, the church and the European government were closely linked together. What affected one affected the other, and therefore, it affected the entire continent. In 1541, Protestant leaders, including Martin Luther, met with the Roman Catholic reformers with the hopes of ironing out their differences.

Discussions were moving along well as the group talked through their beliefs concerning salvation. Both groups agreed that sinners are saved through the death of Christ on the cross and the gift of grace and mercy. Both groups agreed that God's grace justifies the sinner by faith. Everything was going along smoothly until the Catholic reformers demanded that the Pope's power over the whole church be recognized. The Protestants refused, and the meeting ended. The Protestant reformers adopted their new slogan "Each man his own pope" after this meeting.

This slogan became the battle cry of those who took a stand against the power of the Catholic Church. This slogan also struck terror in the hearts of many. What would happen to the worldwide Christian Church if everyone had their own Bible and could read and interpret the Scriptures for themselves? What would happen to the truth? Would the church fall apart, shattered into a thousand separate pieces? Did Christ come just to have His followers divide and turn on each other? And what about the rest of the world? How could a shattered church reach those who were lost? How could reform be good if it was going to lead to the demise of the church?

All of these seemingly valid questions led the Roman Catholic Church leaders to speak out strongly against the Protestants. The Pope condemned the whole group as heretics. Still, the Reformation continued. The awakening in the souls of men seemed as contagious as the Black Death plague, but instead of spreading death and destruction, the Reformation brought hope and light. From this time forward, the Christian church would be divided into denominations.

Nothing of this magnitude happens quietly, though! There were those on both sides of this division, who were motivated by greed. Their reason for division was fueled by selfish gain. A good example of this is when Henry VIII became a Protestant. He was not interested in furthering the cause of the Reformation, he was simply trying to get rid of his wife! Do you recall how he went to the pope to have his marriage to his first wife annulled? The pope said "NO!" and Henry VIII was angry enough to declare himself the Head of the Church of England. By doing this Henry was saying, "I am the king of England, and no Italian pope is going to tell me what to do!"

The Reformation had begun, and the Counter Reformation had responded. This idea of reform in the church, and therefore in the world, would be the fuel for wars for years to come. Country would fight against country, brother against brother. This would become one of the bloodiest eras in history.

Now, let's continue the story of King Henry VIII and his children. In our last chapter, Henry's beloved son, Edward, had died. The sickly boy had become king when he was very young, and by the time he was fifteen years old, Edward was too ill to even leave his bed. News of the sickly King's imminent death spread throughout England. When Edward died, the nation held its breath to see what would happen next. England had never had a ruling queen before; which daughter of Henry VIII would be their ruler?

Narration Break: <u>Discuss the Reformation and the Counter Reformation.</u>

Mary

Mary, the older sister, took the throne in 1553. Elizabeth, the younger sister, was a bit nervous and with good reason! Mary did not like her younger sister. She felt that Elizabeth was a threat to her reign. Queen Mary had her sister arrested on suspicion of plotting against her. Elizabeth was thrown into the Tower of London, where she stayed for months.

Princess Elizabeth, however, was not a vicious and conniving person like her sister, and eventually Queen Mary had to let her leave the tower. After her stay in the tower, Elizabeth was banished to a small cottage in the country. Mary appointed guards to watch her sister's every move and to search the cottage often.

Why was Mary so vicious toward her sister? Think back to the story of King Henry VIII and his many wives. Henry's first wife was Catherine of Aragon,

France. This was Mary's mother and the woman Henry sent away after they had been married for over eighteen years. When her mother was sent away and her parents' marriage was dissolved, everything was taken from Mary. She went from being spoiled "Princess Mary" to "the Lady Mary" overnight. Her place in line to the throne was given to her new, little half-sister Elizabeth, who was the daughter of the current wife of Mary's father, Henry VIII. (Are you confused yet?)

Mary refused to acknowledge her father's second wife as the queen and Elizabeth as the princess. She was so angry with her father, she did not speak to him for over three years. When Mary heard that her mother, Catherine, was ill and dying, Mary was not even allowed to visit her.

When her father's second wife and Katherine's mother, Anne Boleyn, lost her head because of the crazy king, Mary and her little sister were forced to accept Jan Seymour as their new stepmother. After their little half-brother was born, though, both of the girls were demoted to "ladies" as baby Edward became heir to the throne. As you can see, Mary and Elizabeth had a rather rocky childhood. The sisters did have one thing in common; their father had gotten rid of both of their mothers.

When Mary took the throne, one of her top priorities was to eradicate the Protestants from England and return it to being a Catholic nation. Mary's persecution of those who left the Roman Catholic Church was extremely severe. The Protestants gave her the name "Bloody Mary" because of the persecution.

The Marion Persecution, as this time period would be called by later historians, was so severe, that more than two hundred eighty Protestants were burned alive. These martyrs were burned at the stake for not obeying Queen Mary's orders to support the Catholic Church. Thousands of other believers were also ushered into the presence of Jesus through her cruel punishment. This was a very dark period of history in England.

Queen Mary wanted to be sure that her Protestant sister, Elizabeth, would not take the throne after her. She decided to marry a distant cousin, Prince Philip of Spain. The couple were wed on July 25, 1554, and soon the happy news of a coming baby spread throughout the kingdom. Queen Mary was going to have an heir to the throne. Nine months came and went, and no baby was born. This happened twice, and even though Mary was exhibiting all of the signs of pregnancy, there was never a baby born. How strange! Each time these instances of "false pregnancy" occurred, Mary became weaker and more ill. Finally, in 1558, at the age of 42, Mary died, leaving no heir to the throne. Modern medicine would have probably revealed that the queen had cancer, which would have caused all of the symptoms mistaken for pregnancy.

As the news of the queen's death spread throughout the kingdom, Elizabeth was brought to the throne. People danced and sang in the streets. Queen Mary had not been a good queen; her cruelty to anyone who dared oppose her terrified her subjects. Unlike her sister, Elizabeth was supportive of the Protestants' cause. She allowed both Catholics and Protestants to worship the way they chose. This was the beginning of a peaceful time for the Protestants of England.

When Elizabeth came to the throne, she changed everything. She replaced all of her sister's servants and advisors. She planned a huge ceremony for her crowning, and the English citizens flocked to the square to celebrate. They called their new queen "Good Queen Bess."

Elizabeth was now Elizabeth I, and her reign would last forty-five years. (This is called the Elizabethan Age.) Elizabeth was a much better queen than her sister. She wanted her people to love her, not be terrified of her. Under her reign, England became stronger, richer, and much more influential than ever before.

Elizabeth

Good Queen Bess determined not to marry. She believed she could do a good job ruling by herself, and she did not want the power going to someone else. Philip, the Spanish prince who had married Queen Mary, was now the Spanish king and offered to marry Elizabeth, but she steadfastly refused.

After Elizabeth refused to marry Philip, he returned to Spain and his throne there. He was already having trouble keeping order in his own kingdom, and he certainly didn't need to deal with his "stubborn" sister-in-law! However, he would soon find out that England was still causing him problems. It seemed on every front, he kept having to deal with the English interference.

In the New World, the English Explorers were finding and claiming lands, which Philip wanted for Spain. On the seas, English slave ships were passing through Spain's waterways on their way to Africa. And English ships were causing trouble for the Spanish gold-transporting business. Philip was getting hot under the collar! He sent a message to Queen Elizabeth warning her not to continue any of these maddening activities. Elizabeth, not wishing to get into a war with the very powerful country of Spain, replied with a peaceful promise to abide by his wishes. In reality, however, Good Queen Bess had no intentions whatsoever of stopping her countrymen's actions. She secretly let her sailors know that they could continue their gold pirating ways, and she continued to send explorers to the Americas.

Soon King Philip realized she had not meant a single word of her peaceful reply. His response to this was to build a monstrously huge floating army. The ships would be massive compared to England's ships, and he planned to use them to overwhelm England's ships. This floating army was called the Spanish Armada, and it was one hundred thirty ships strong! When the Armada came into the English Channel, however, the English were prepared. Their ships were much smaller and faster

than the floating fortresses of the Armada. The English warships sailed circles around the massive Spanish ships, shooting holes up and down the sides. Even though the Spanish outnumbered the English two to one, the agility of the English warships proved to be too much for the Armada. Seventy of the Spanish ships were destroyed and twenty thousand soldiers killed. England had won the battle, and from that point on, she would be known for the strength of her navy.

Narration Break: Retell the story of Queens Mary and Elizabeth Tudor.

Chapter 24

Science and Philosophy of the Middle Ages

To understand the world of science in the Middle Ages, we must go much further back in time to the Ancients. Written records from around 3,000 B.C. show us that the Ancient Egyptians had a relatively sophisticated medical understanding for that time period; although, in reality, their medical practice was limited to trial and error. They might do something that worked, but they didn't know why it worked. For example, they knew that laying a piece of moldy bread on a wound would keep the patient from developing an infection, but they had no idea that it was because the mold produced penicillin, a chemical that kills infections and germs. Another amazing example of the Egyptians' medical ingenuity was how they used seeds from a poppy flower for pain medication. We know today that these seeds contain codeine and morphine, two powerful pain relievers.

Also, in the headlines of the Ancient science times are the Egyptian invention of papyrus paper, the Mesopotamian invention of the wheel, and the Chinese invention and use of the compass. All of these inventions may sound commonplace and unexciting to us, but they revolutionized the Ancient world. The wheel made it possible to have horse-drawn carriages and carts, which of course, completely changed the modes of travel and the fighting methods.

All of these discoveries and inventions are wonderful indeed, but could they really be classified as "true science"? Science is collecting data and facts, organizing them, observing them, and trying to explain them. What these people did was helpful, but was it really science? What do you think? As far as we can tell from the histories left by the ancient civilizations, the Greeks were really the first true scientists. From these records, we know that a man known as Thales studied the heavens and came up with theories about the movement of the stars. He was able to predict a solar eclipse, which made him famous all over the known world. These celestial events had previously thrown everyone into an absolute panic! It was wonderful to be able to understand what was going on.

Statue of Thales

The second well-known Greek scientist was a student of Thales. Anaximander (an-AXE-uh-man-der) was more interested in the study of life, or rather, the origins of life. As far as we know, Anaximander was the first scientist who tried to come up with an origin of life which excluded a Creator. This is the theory that was later revived by a man named Charles Darwin and would become the seed of evolution, a theory that still plagues the earth today.

Statue of Anaximander

The third of the trio was

Anaximenes (an-AXE-uh-ME-nees).
Anaximander and Anaximenes were
probably co-workers.   While
Anaximander erroneously tried to figure
out the origins of life, Anaximenes tried
to find the most basic element or
substance in the world.   His conclusion?
Air.   Although he was wrong in his
conclusion, Anaximenes was on the right
track.   It was his idea about air that led
to the later discovery of the atom.

Statue of Anaximenes

There were other important Greek scientists, who lived between 600 BC and 100 AD, but we are only going to take the time to study one of them. I believe that we should include Aristotle (air-uh-STOT-le) in our study, because his teaching would affect the world all the way through the 1800s! Aristotle had a vast amount of influence on the world of science. I believe the most profound, positive contribution Aristotle gave to the world of science was the idea of classification. If you read Volume 4 of this series, you will remember the story of Alexander the Great. Aristotle lived during that time period and received financial backing from Alexander the Great. Because of this, Aristotle was able to obtain specimens of flora and fauna, from all over the known world, to add to his classification system.

Perhaps one of the most influential of Aristotle's ideas was spontaneous generation. This absolutely ridiculous idea stated that something could be generated from nothing. For example, maggots could be brought into existence from raw meat without the presence of a fly. Now, you might think that this is ridiculous because you need a fly to lay an egg, which would hatch out a maggot, which is a fly in the larva stage, and you would be right! You might be as surprised as I am to know that the general population actually believed this idea. Because people knew that maggots were found in or near raw meat, they thought that this great, thinking man, Aristotle, had discovered a great scientific fact. Aristotle was considered one of the greatest scientists of his day, and in a way, he was. Although many of his ideas were not quite factual, he did advance many other ideas for science.

Narration Break: _Discuss each scientist we have learned about. How did the Ancient Egyptians "do science"?_

During the Middle Ages, the Catholic Church revered Aristotle to the point of making him a saint. We have learned that during this time period, the line between church and the government were so blurred; sometimes they each used the power of the other to control the masses. We have also learned that these years are called the Dark Ages because many people did not have the light of education, the written Word of God, or a very hope-filled lifestyle. In many areas all over the Eastern Hemisphere, the very rich oppressed and ruled over the poor using the Feudal System. Above it all, the church had risen to incredible, disproportionate power.

These dark years greatly affected the world of science. Science and discovery mostly came to a grinding halt. The church held the position that Aristotle's teachings were untouchable, and anyone who might question his teachings was considered a heretic. However, as much as the church and the government squelched scientific advancement, they also can be thanked for keeping the records of all of the scientific discoveries from the ages before.

Monks, the same men whom we learned copied the Scriptures by hand, also copied the accumulated scientific knowledge. It was because of their diligence, the next age of history was able to make huge scientific advances.

So what kinds of discoveries and inventions did scientists do during the Middle Ages? Were there scientists at all? During the roughly fifteen hundred years of the Middle Ages, the scientists were mainly what we call alchemists (AL-kuh-mists). These "scientists" tried to make precious metals or liquids by combining other substances. For example, one of the alchemists' dearest desires was to transform lead, or any other common metal, into gold by mixing it with other substances. They had witnessed chemical reactions before and the substance left behind after the reaction, so the alchemists spent months trying different combinations.

Like the Ancient Egyptians before them, the alchemists operated mostly by trial and error. Whenever they happened to create a useful substance from their experiments, they wrote down the "recipe." Although they never discovered any metals to make gold - God alone holds that recipe - they did concoct some helpful substances.

One area of scientific advancement did occur in the Middle Ages. It was during this time period, the Chinese made many accurate observations of the heavenly bodies. The Chinese astronomers, who were familiar with the stars and constellations, were the first to notice changes, either appearances or disappearances, of those stars. In fact, they kept such impressive records that hundreds of years later, scientists were able to study these Chinese writings and conclude what the Chinese had seen - a supernova, an exploding star. I find this fascinating! We will learn more about the astronomical discoveries of the Renaissance period in a later chapter, but please remember how the Chinese were very helpful with their carefully documented observations of the sky.

The study of the scientists of the Middle Ages easily flows into a look at the philosophers of this time period as well. Science and philosophy have always walked through history hand in hand - both fields of study scrutinize the what and why of the physical world and the human ability to understand it. We have learned that many of the ancient scientists were highly revered throughout the Middle Ages, and the same is true for the ancient philosophers.

Socrates was a philosopher of Ancient Greece. His teachings about the search for knowledge, both what it is and how it can be acquired, were highly revered by several of his students, who in turn wrote extensively about them. Socrates also studied and taught about logic, and even though it was Aristotle, who is attributed with establishing logic as a formal discipline in education, Socrates also is considered one of its leading teachers. One of Socrates' students, Plato, who became the teacher of the much revered Aristotle, was also

Plato

influential to the study of philosophy.

Socrates, Plato, and Aristotle had all taught to analyze, debate, and categorize information in a logical order. They taught that education is an art and a science, which is broken down into steps - a process - which the human mind uses to acquire knowledge. They taught that these mental processes are recognize, recall, analyze, reflect, apply, create, understand, and evaluate. (The establishing and recognition of this process was hugely influential on the developing Western Civilization and is still recognized and used to teach today.)

As the Middle Ages dawned on history, the teachings of these revered philosophers were still preserved and cultivated, but slowly, there was another element being added and mixed with it; Christian theology was becoming part of the philosophical thinking of the day. The secular philosophy of Socrates, Plato, and Aristotle was slowly being replaced by theological ideas.

One of the most noted "thinkers" of the Middle Ages was Thomas Aquinas. (We learned about him back in Chapter 14.) Even though Thomas never considered himself a philosopher, he was extremely influential on the world of philosophy. Thomas criticized philosophers for completely missing the point of thinking and seeking wisdom. This gentle monk knew this truth: Wisdom is a gift from God, and like Proverbs 1:7 says, "The fear of the LORD is the beginning of knowledge." Thomas believed in worshipping and serving God, the Maker of his brain and his ability to understand, instead of worshipping himself.

Narration Break: Discuss the affect the Ancient "thinkers" had on the Middle Ages. What happened as time went on?

Chapter 25

Copernicus, Galileo, and Shakespeare

Have you ever heard the saying, "_____ thinks they are the center of the universe"? This expression means that the party in question thinks they are more important than others around them. The connotations are rather negative, usually expressing self-centeredness. However, the belief that the earth is the center of the universe was widely accepted during the Middle Ages.

In our last chapter about science and philosophy of the Middle Ages, we learned how the Ancient scientists and philosophers greatly influenced the world for a long time. In this chapter, I want to tell you about another man from the Ancient days, who had an amazing influence on the world for an incredibly long time. Ptolemy was an astronomer and geographer from Egypt, under the Greek rule. Ptolemy taught that our planet Earth was at the very center of our universe. This theory is called the geocentric universe. The prefix "geo" means "earth," and the words "centric" means "in the center." Thus geocentric literally means "Earth in the center."

For many hundreds of years, the geocentric view was considered sacred. According to the Roman Catholic Church, Ptolemy was 100% accurate, because surely humans, the most important of all God's creation, would be placed at the center of the universe. So, you see, it really wasn't anything about science; it was about preconceived ideas. Why would everyone just accept this theory without question?

If you go outside and look up at the sky, can you tell the earth is spinning at a rate of about one thousand miles per hour? One spin all the way around its axis equals one day. When you go outside in the winter, you probably notice that the sun is lower in the sky. (This is especially true and noticeable if you live far north in the Northern Hemisphere.) By looking at the sky, can you tell you are at a different place in our year-long trip around the sun? Probably not! If you did not *know* that our planet travels around the sun, you would easily believe that it is the earth at the center of the universe. The sun does appear to be traveling around us, therefore it is an understandable mistake.

There were all types of odd but understandable ideas and theories about the universe during the Ancient and Middle Ages. One of these theories included a giant turtle carrying the flat, plate-like Earth on its back. Some believed that the sun exploded into millions of pieces each night, thus making the glittering, twinkling stars. Most of the Ancient civilizations had legends and lore involving the celestial bodies.

During the 16th and 17th centuries, several scientists made some extremely exciting and important discoveries. In 1543, a man named Nicolaus Copernicus published a book outlining his findings concerning the heavens. Copernicus' book caused quite a stir! For the first time, a scientist was disputing the geocentric universe theory.

Instead of the earth being in the center, Copernicus argued that the sun was in the center, with the planets, including the earth, circling around it. This book very quickly became one of the Roman Catholic Church's top banned books. Copernicus was right, of course, but his book was not extremely popular. You see, he had drawn the conclusion of a heliocentric (sun in the center) universe, not

because of a big stack of evidence *for* the new theory, but because of all of the evidence *against* the geocentric theory.

Most of us need a lot of evidence to make us change our minds about something that seems so obvious to us. Copernicus wasn't able to provide this evidence. It would take a few more years and another scientist's pen to make this evidence available. In the late 1500s, a man named Johannes Kepler began observing the heavens. Kepler, a teacher, who yearned to be a minister, liked the stars. As his observations began to interest him more and more,

Kepler decided to document what he was seeing.

Johannes Kepler kept such detailed, accurate drawings that he was able to track the orbits of the planets around the sun. He used mathematical equations to predict and chart the planets' movements. These equations became known as "Kepler's Laws," and they became extremely important to the world of astronomy. They were also instrumental in the heliocentric versus the geocentric argument.

Kepler

A few years later, in the early 1600s, another scientist named Galileo helped bring even more evidence of a heliocentric universe. Galileo actually built a telescope, with which he was able to study the movements of the planets with amazing accuracy.

The Roman Catholic Church did not appreciate Galileo's work, however! They arrested him for heresy and put him on trial. Galileo was a good Catholic, and when they demanded that he recant the heliocentric universe theory, he obliged; however, he continued gathering information and evidence supporting it. Eventually, there was so much evidence supporting it, the Catholic Church was forced to accept the heliocentric universe theory.

Narration Break: Narrate the story of Copernicus and Galileo.

In the years of Good Queen Bess, England became a land of cultural prominence. Artists painted beautiful masterpieces, composers wrote exquisite music, and playwrights penned famous theatricals. Of all the English playwrights ever to write plays, one stands head and shoulders above the rest. The name of Shakespeare is familiar to virtually every ear since the 1500s.

William Shakespeare was born six years after Queen Elizabeth came to the throne. William started acting at a young age, and soon he had a troupe of actors working with him.

Shakespeare acted, helped with costumes, and wrote the plays for the troupe, who called themselves "Lord Chamberlain's Men." They traveled around England, performing at inns and in courtyards. Eventually, they performed in the Globe Theatre, a large outdoor theater with rows of balconies, which enabled the audience an unobstructed view of the play.

The plays William wrote made people laugh and cry; he wrote comedies and historical dramas. He performed for rich people and for poor people, and soon, William's name was on everyone's lips. Queen Elizabeth even called on William Shakespeare to perform for her. Shakespeare's plays are still played today. They have been published in books and made into movies. Out of all of the playwrights in history, William Shakespeare's plays are undoubtedly some of the most famous and performed of all times.

If you own any of Shakespeare's plays (even simplified or abridged versions will work), take the time now to read some. If you do not own any, there are many websites that offer readers a chance to read the original, unabridged versions of Shakespeare's plays at no charge.

Narration Break: Discuss the last part of our chapter.

Chapter 26

Art and Artists of the Middle Ages

Parents: please note that much of the art from this time period includes a fair bit of nudity. Please preview all art searches. (Learned from experience!)

In this chapter, we are going to take a look at some of the art of the Middle Ages, and at some of the great artists of that day. We have learned that the church and the government of that time were so closely intertwined that it is sometimes difficult, if not impossible, to separate the two. The church held high importance in the culture, as well as much power in the government. The art of the Middle Ages reflects this fact.

We will take a look at several artists from the Middle Ages. When you think about artists, you might think of rich, influential people, who are famous and admired by their peers. It might surprise you to know that many of the artists of the Middle Ages were actually simple, unassuming monks, and much of the artwork was focused on the life of Jesus, the early saints, or other important, church-related topics.

The first artist we will learn about was named Giotto (Lived: 1266 - 1337). As a young boy, Giotto was a simple shepherd boy. One day, as he was tending his flocks, he drew a picture on a piece of slate with a sharp stone. It so happened that an artist name Cimabue (chee-ma-BOO-ay) was passing by and watched in amazement as Giotto sketched away with his primitive artist's tools. Cimabue was so impressed that he offered to take Giotto to Florence, Italy, in order to give him a chance to learn about art. Giotto's parents were delighted to give their approval.

Artists of this time did not have the wonderfully diverse array of creative mediums available to them like we do now. Instead, they mixed their paint powders with water to create frescos (which means "fresh") on freshly plastered walls. If they wanted their paint to be sticky, they mixed their paint powder with egg. When they did this, they were able to paint on dried plaster or wood. They called this type of painting "tempera" which means "mixed."

Giotto

If you study the artwork from this time period, you will notice how "flat" they appear. This is because Giotto and other artists painted without using perspective. They had not discovered how to make objects look farther away behind the main focus of their picture. In other words, their pictures had no depth. All of the characters were simply lined up across the painting, much like the ancient tomb paintings of the Egyptians.

Masaccio

This problem with perspective was solved by a very young, poor artist named Masaccio (Ma-ZAT-cho), which is actually quite an insulting nickname. (You see, Masaccio means "Dirty Tom" in Italian.) Masaccio died at the young age of twenty-six, and while he was alive, no one seemed to care for his paintings at all. In fact, his paintings were never studied or even looked at by other artists until after his untimely death. After his passing, however, many artists thought his paintings were so good, they decided to take them to study his techniques. The artists were intrigued at how they felt like they could almost walk into Masaccio's paintings. These artists started trying to add this dimension of perspective to their own paintings.

Perhaps one of the most well-known artists of the Middle Ages was actually born during what we call the Renaissance, in the year 1475. I am sure that many of you hearing or reading this story have heard the name Michelangelo, the famous artist who painted the ceiling of the Sistine Chapel in Rome, Italy. Michelangelo's full name was Michelangelo di Lodovico Buonarroti Simoni - a good, solid Italian name!

Michelangelo considered himself a sculptor, not a painter, but when the pope asked him to create paintings depicting famous stories from the Bible, Michelangelo decided he would prove he was a painter, too. The only way he could paint was to lie on his back on scaffolding, built close to the ceiling; it took him four and a half years to complete this mammoth project. Because he was a sculptor, he painted the men and women in the Bible story scenes to look like sculptures. We call this type of painting "sculpturesque."

Another famous artist from the Renaissance period is also considered one of the outstanding scientists of the time period. Leonardo da Vinci (1452-1519), the creator of the famous painting, the _Mona Lisa_, is also known for his study of the human body. Perhaps this is why his paintings are so extremely well proportioned and realistic. Leonardo was extremely intelligent. His interests in music, mathematics, science, painting, geology, botany, and even writing, led him to be much sought after by many important people.

The next two artists we are going to meet worked together to found the Venetian school of Italian Renaissance Painting. Giorgione Barbarelli da Castelfranco (1477-1510), who went only by his first name, thankfully, was known for his "poetic" style of painting. Not much is known about Giorgione (shgee-or-GO-nee), and only six pieces of his work remain. We do know, through written accounts about him, that he was a significant influence on the world of Renaissance art. We also know that he was the the teacher of Titian

(TISH-un) (c.1488 - 1576), also known as Tiziano Vecelli, another Italian painter. Titian is known for his use of color in particular and his style of painting - specifically the type of brush stroke he used. Titian had much influence on the future generations of artists.

Our last artist is a Spanish artist named Diego Rodriguez de Silva y Velazquez (1599-1660). Diego Rodriguez was an artist of the early Baroque period, who was known for his ability to paint portraits. His ability to paint realistic likenesses endeared him to the Spanish royal family, and Diego painted dozens of portraits for them. He also painted beautiful depictions of historical happenings. In many ways, Diego Rodriguez ushered in a new type of art. His paintings are so realistic and individualized, they are simply breathtaking! (As a side note, one of the aspects I personally appreciate about Rodriguez's paintings is the fact that the subjects are usually fully clothed!) Diego Rodriguez's work would become a model for the painters of the later time periods.

* * * * * * * * * * * * * * * * * * *

Paintings and frescos of the Middle Ages and Renaissance are extremely distinctive. Their style is easy to differentiate from other time periods because of the use of certain color pallets and hard edges. As you study the art pieces of Masaccio, Giotto, and Michelangelo on the next two pages, notice the way the figures appear to be almost outlined in a darker color. Even though the faces and figures are realistic in the sense they do not look like cartoons, there is something about them that does not look realistic. Next, study the work done by Titian and Diego Rodriguez and discuss the differences you see.

If you would like to explore more artists from this time period, here are some to get you started:

- Fra Angelico

- Rembrandt

- Van Eyck

- Dürer

Adoration of the Shepherds 1508 by Giorgione

Christ and the Cyrenian by Titian

The title of this painting is "Crucifixion." Giotto painted it in 1306.

Study of a Woman's Head
Leonardo da Vinci

221

The Tribute Money, by Masaccio   Notice how the artist used dimension.

The Creation of Adam 1512
Part of the Sistine Chapel ceiling
by Michelangelo

An Old Woman Frying Eggs
Diego Rodriguez

Chapter 27

Music of the Middle Ages

There has been music in the world almost since the beginning of time. During the Middle Ages, music was largely influenced by the Catholic Church, and "sacred" music was most prevalent. One of the earliest types of music during this time was the Gregorian Chant. We must remember that the early Middle Ages was not too far removed from Bible times, so the traditional Jewish chants were still used. A chant isn't really a song, but it was used as one during church services and other times of worship. It is believed that Pope Gregory I organized and established uniform usage of the chants throughout the Catholic Church in the west, sometime in the late 590s or early 600s.

Don't confuse these chants with what modern music calls "rap." Chants were something entirely different! These chants were more like a drone - a single melody without any harmony or accompaniment. The words were droned slowly and slipped from major to minor scales and back again. Many of these chants were sections of Scriptures, which were memorized in whole chapters.

Not all music was written by and performed at church. Do you recall how we learned that much of the history of the Middle Ages was sung by minstrels? These songs were not chants at all but more like folk songs. They were usually song by one person who played a stringed instrument for accompaniment. These minstrels made their living by traveling around from village to village, singing for their supper and lodging. Many of these songs never made it to paper, but we do know that most minstrels had one main tune, to which they changed words to tell the current events of the day.

There were other types of ethnic music during the Middle Ages. The Celts had their own music, as well as the Vikings and the countries of the Orient and other parts of Asia. Their music and songs told the epic tales of how their countries were forming, and sad tales of battles, and romantic songs of love. Each type of music had its own type of melody and harmony, and each had its own place in its respective culture.

It wasn't until around 1300 that a music composer actually wrote his music, performed it, and had it formally preserved for future generations. This musician and poet was named Guillaume de Machaut. It seems that this man was the first composer of polyphonic music. Polyphonic means music written for more than one voice to sing and more than one instrument to play at a time. Machaut was much sought after by many important people of Europe, and his music was well-known all over the civilized world.

Here is a sample verse from one of Machaut's poems. (Translation credit to Google Translate™)

Puis qu'en oubli sui de vous, dous amis.
Vie amoureuse et joie a Dieu commant.
Mar vi le jour que m'amour en vous mis.
Puis qu'en oubli sui de vous, dous amis.
Mais ce tenray que je vous ay promis.
C'est que ja mais n'aray nul autre amant.
Puis qu'en oubli sui de vous, dous amis.
Vie amoureuse et joie a Dieu commant.

Then forget that following you, dous friends.
Love life and joy commant God.
March vi day that you love me made.
Then forget that following you, dous friends.
But tenray that I have promised you.
Is that ja aray but no other lover.
Then forget that following you, dous friends.
Love life and joy commant God.

Chapter 27

Just as the Renaissance was a time of rebirth in science, philosophy, and the arts throughout Europe, it was also a time of awakening in music. The renewed interest in the writings of ancient Greece and Rome had led to a renewed interest in learning across the culture. When the printing press came along, books and written music were much more readily available. With Martin Luther's Protestant Reformation and Copernicus and Kepler's discovery of the actual position of the earth in the solar system, the Catholic Church lost its grip on society. This new way of thinking manifested itself in the plays of Shakespeare, the painting and sculptures of Michelangelo, and in both the sacred and secular dance and vocal music of the greatest composers of the era.

Throughout the Renaissance, instrumental dance music was "composed," by many types of people. This type of music was often made up at the spur of the moment whenever the need arose. Musicians collected much of this music and published it in various volumes through the years. The dance music of Tielman Susato (1500-1561) and "The Terpsichore" by Michael Praetorius (1571-1621) give us an example of the dance music from the late Renaissance. Josquin des Prez is attributed with a piece called La Spagna, which is an excellent example of the bouncy rhythms and sounds of the Renaissance dance. Many of these dance forms were used later by composers and found their way into the Baroque dance suite.

Not much is known about the life of Josquin des Prez, but it is believed that he studied under the early Renaissance master, Johannes Ockeghem (1420-1495), the first great master at the Flemish School of Renaissance Composers. It appears that Josquin served at several courts in Italy and

France and even at the Sistine Chapel in Rome, and he died while serving as canon of the church at Condé.

The peaceful, heavenly choral sound of the Flemish School's style can be heard in the "Gloria" from Josquin's "Missa L'homme Armé." The coinciding mixing of several melodic lines, most usually soprano, alto, tenor, bass, in a musical composition, is known as polyphony. Polyphonic music of the Renaissance could be very complex and intricate. It sometimes obscured the words and the meaning of the text, which had been set to music.

Narration Break: Discuss the music of the Middle Ages. Look for music samples.

The Polyphonic music was the kind of music the later, great composers used as a starting place for their famous compositions. One of these composers was Johann Sebastian Bach, a German composer from the Baroque period of music. Bach was born in the year 1685 to an abundantly musical family. Bach's father, Johann Ambrosius, played the violin and taught Johann Sebastian the instrument as well. He learned to play the organ, clavichord, and harpsichord from his brother, Johann Christoph.

Johann Sebastian's childhood was a happy one until his parents died when he was nearly ten years old. He and his thirteen year old brother, Josef, went to live with their older brother, Christoph and his wife. When he was fifteen years old, Johann Sebastian went to Lüneberg to become a choirboy at St. Michael's Church. In his lifetime, Johann Sebastian Bach wrote hundreds of beautiful compositions to play at his church. This quiet, unassuming man had no interest in garnishing applause from the crowds; he simply played his music because he loved it, and he loved God. No one thought of him as a great composer until after he died. Many years after Bach's death, Felix Mendelssohn discovered the beautiful compositions and wanted others to hear them, so he organized Johann Sebastian's compositions into sixty volumes of music. As Mendelssohn read through Bach's compositions, he noticed the lettering "*SDG*" on many of the pages. Soli Deo Gloria, "To God alone be the glory," had been the quiet, heartfelt praise of this man, who left so many breathtaking hymns and anthems for us to sing. A close-to-literal translation of the original German.

Jesu, Joy of Man's Desiring:

Well for me that I have Jesus,
O how strong I hold to him
that he might refresh my heart,
when sick and sad am I.
Jesus have I, who loves me
and gives to me his own,
ah, therefore I will not leave Jesus,
when I feel my heart is breaking.

Jesus remains my joy,
my heart's comfort and essence,
Jesus resists all suffering,
He is my life's strength,
my eye's desire and sun,
my soul's love and joy;
so will I not leave Jesus
out of heart and face.

Let's look at one more of the Baroque period composers. Antonio Lucio Vivaldi (1678 – 1741) was nicknamed "The Red Priest" (il Prete Rosso), because he had red hair. Vivaldi was an Italian Baroque composer, Catholic priest, and virtuoso violinist. He is recognized as one of the greatest Baroque composers, and during his lifetime, his influence was widespread all over Europe. Vivaldi is known for composing instrumental concertos, many especially for the violin. He also wrote over forty operas and sacred choral works. His best-known work is a series of violin concertos known as *The Four Seasons*.

Like Bach, Vivaldi wrote many of his music ensembles for noble purposes. He had been employed at a home for abandoned children, and he composed many musical scores for the nuns, who worked there, to sing to the children. Because of this, many of his compositions are written for women to sing. Vivaldi is ranked amongst the most popular and widely-recorded of all composers of the Baroque period.

There are far too many composers of wonderful music from the Middle Ages. From Celtic bards to Japanese folk songs, the music was as varied as the cultures of the countries from which they came. This study of the music of the Middle Ages is meant only to whet your appetite for discovery. I highly recommend that you study some of the hymns and hymn writers of this time and the time directly following the Renaissance.

Narration Break: <u>Discuss the stories of Bach and Vivaldi.</u>

Sometime this week, make sure you listen to some samples of music from the Middle Ages, Renaissance, and the Baroque Period. Enjoy!

Here is an old hymn, which has been revised in recent years. These are the original words, complete with their original spelling.

God be in My Hede

from the Sarum Primer, 1558

God be in my hede
And in my understandyng
God by myne eyes
And in my lokyng,
God be in my mouth
And in my speakyng,
God be in my harte
And in my thinkyng
God be at myne end
And in my departyng.

Here is the revised:

God be in my head, and in my understanding;
God be in mine eyes, and in my looking;
God be in my mouth, and in my speaking;
God be in my heart, and in my thinking;
God be at mine end, and at my departing.

Chapter 28

How the Renaissance Affected the World
& Mary Queen of Sots and Her Son, James

As our study of the Middle Ages draws to a close, let's take the time to review and summarize how the world has changed over the course of the fifteen centuries since our Lord Jesus walked the earth. When Christ was born and lived here on this planet, the Roman Empire was the leading world power. Their empire was so far flung, virtually every civilization in the Eastern Hemisphere was affected by the influence of the Roman culture. When the Roman Empire split and finally fell, the crash shook the entire continent of Europe. What followed that crash was considered one of the darkest times in the history of the world.

As we moved from the Dark Ages into the time of the Reformation and the Renaissance, we watched cultures change. The darkness of illiteracy began to fade away, as books became more readily available to the common man. Men dedicated to the translating of the Bible into common, readable languages and the invention of the printing press enabled the light of truth to spread. As the darkness lost its grip on Europe, the Roman Catholic Church also was forced to loosen their control.

Advances in science, technology, literature, music, and religious freedoms fanned the blaze of curiosity and exploration all over the Eastern Hemisphere. By the sixteenth century, virtually every European country had their explorations in the New World. Many of them had claimed large tracts of land for their mother countries. A new age of exploration and settlement had begun.

This flame of curiosity had, at first, flickered dimly, a tiny ember in the darkest night, and then, as one solitary person after another stepped forth to insist on the truth, the fire sputtered and leapt until it was a raging inferno, sweeping with unstoppable fury through the hearts of mankind.

Before our story is completely over, I would like us to learn about a king who was responsible for giving us the King James Version of the Bible. We learned about how the daughters of King Henry VIII, Mary and Elizabeth Tudor, were the queens of England. Mary, known for her cruelty to Protestants, did not leave an heir to the throne when she died after being queen for only five

years. After her sister's death, Elizabeth came to the throne, and for forty-five years, she was a good queen, well loved by her subjects. Around this time, a cousin of Mary and Elizabeth Tudor lived in Scotland.

The story of Mary, Queen of Scots, has been made into plays and musicals for many years, because it is a very interesting story. Mary, Queen of Scots, was the niece of Henry VIII, and she was also the mother of the King James who authorized the version of the Bible that many of us use today (although it has been updated with a bit more modern English!).

Mary, Queen of Scots, was born Mary Stuart. Her father was King James V of Scotland. James V was the son of Margaret Tudor, who was the sister of King Henry VIII. Queen Elizabeth I (also known as Good Queen Bess) had her cousin Mary, Queen of Scots, incarcerated and eventually executed when evidence showed Mary was in on an assignation plot against Elizabeth.

As the Tudor sisters were on the throne of England (who ruled Ireland at this time), the country of Scotland had its own ruler, but when Elizabeth I of England died, leaving no heir to the throne, James, the king of Scotland, who was her first cousin twice removed became the king of Scotland, England, and Ireland. I know that all of this can become quite confusing, but try to remember this: when James became king of all three nations, this was called the "Union of the Crowns" or the "Treaty of Union," which happened in March 1603. England and Scotland did not want to become one nation, and it was not until 1706-1707 that the separate Parliaments of Scotland and England agreed to become Great Britain.

In our next volume of history, we are going to take an in depth look at the exploration and settlement of the New World. It was because of the Renaissance this exploration happened. The new way of thinking drove the curious-minded people to expand their borders, to push against the known, to think outside of the box, which had been their comfort zone for so many years. As we close our study of the Middle Ages, I encourage you to dig in deeper! Discover more about each of the aspects of this time period. Listen to the music, study the artwork, and read the literature.

Narration Break: Discuss your favorite part of the story of the Middle Ages.

Chapter 28

Please leave blank

Appendix Title Page

- Deeper Research Topics
- Optional Lesson Plans
- Tips for Struggling Learners
- Works Cited

Please leave blank

A Closer Look

Chapter 1:

Research and write a short report about Josephus. Expound on why he has been a controversial figure in Christian history.

Chapter 2:

Research the Edict of Milan. What affects did it have on history?

Chapter 3:

Who are the current leaders of China, Japan, and Korea (North and South)?

Chapter 4:

Research the Mayan calendar. What affect has this civilization's "science" had on the world?

Chapter 5:

What kind of lifestyle and culture did the Celts of Britain have directly following the fall of the Roman Empire?

Chapter 6:

Research Hadrian's Wall. What was it? Learn more about why it was built.

Chapter 7:

See if you can find actual blue prints for a castle. Do they differ from country to country/century to century?

Chapter 8:

Read a story about a Muslim who converted to Christianity. What kind of life do they lead now, and how hard was life following their conversion.

Chapter 9:

Do some deeper research into the Battle of Tours.

Chapter 10:

The Vikings left behind something called the Rune Stones. What are they? Do some research about them!

Chapter 11:

Do some deeper research on the Easter Island Heads.

Chapter 12:

Research the People's Crusade. Write a short essay about what you find.

Chapter 13:

Research the Minstrel, Blondel. This is the minstrel most often credited with finding the kidnapped Richard the Lionhearted.

Lesson 14:

Research the modern city of Beijing. Find some pictures and information and write a short report.

Chapter 15:

Find the origin of the word "Kamikaze." Where did this word originate? What does it mean?

Chapter 16:

Find out more about Mansa Musa, the most powerful of all Mali leaders.

Chapter 17:

Even today, John Wycliffe is revered by Bible Translators world-wide. Find out more about his influence.

Chapter 18:

What other doors of discovery did the printing press open?

Chapter 19:

Ivan the Great was considered the first czar of Russia. Who was the last? What king of government did the Czars represent?

Chapter 20:

What other events happened in Spain under the rule of Ferdinand and Isabella? Do some research and write a short report about the most important events.

Chapter 21:

Did Martin Luther ever debate Tetzel? Try to find out and write about it.

Chapter 22:

Henry VIII was responsible for the English split from the Roman Catholic Church. Find out more about this, and write a few paragraphs telling why he split and what happened to the Church of England after this event.

Chapter 23:

Find out more about the fight between France and England over the waterways in the Atlantic Ocean.

Chapter 24:

Why do you think Aristotle's idea of Spontaneous Generation was held so highly for so long? for what good contributions can we thank Aristotle?

Chapter 25:

Read more about the geocentric universe theory. In this theory, where exactly was the sun's supposed position in the universe?

Chapter 26:

What are the different art periods? What is your favorite? Find some samples.

Chapter 27:

Johann Sebastian Bach was a very godly man. What other hymns did he compose?

Chapter 28:

What other ways did the Renaissance way of thinking affect the world?

	Level 1 - early elementary	Level 2 - middle to upper elementary	Level 3 - Jr. High	Level 4 - Sr. High
Day 1	Listen to the first part of story, narrate orally & work on Journal pages	Listen to the first part of story, narrate orally & work on Journal pages	Listen to/read the story Work on Journal pages	Listen to/read the story Work on Journal pages
Day 2	Listen to the last part of story, narrate orally & work on Journal pages	Listen to the last part of story, narrate orally & work on Journal pages	Listen to/read the story Work on Journal pages	Listen to/read the story Work on Journal pages
Day 3	Complete timeline project and review chapter	Complete timeline project and review chapter Do written narration prompts	Do written narration prompts (optional) Complete timeline project and review chapter	Do written narration prompts (optional) Complete timeline project and review chapter
Day 4	Optional: hands-on projects	Optional: hands-on projects	Optional: Do hands-on project	Optional: Do hands-on project
Throughout week			Use Jr. High Level research packet to do deeper research topic Optional - Read assigned literature	Use Sr. High level research packet to do deeper research topic Optional - Read assigned literature

- Review 1 after Chapter 7.
- Review 2 after Chapter 14.
- Review 3 after Chapter 21.
- Final Review, followed by family show and tell night, after Chapter 28.

Review Activities Suggestions

- Make posters showing your favorite part of a chapter.
- Create a replica of a home or clothing article from the time period and ethnic group you are studying about.
- At the end of your review week, hold a show-and-tell for your family and friends.
- Cook a meal that goes with your time period and civilization.
- Listen to authentic ethnic music.
- Look at authentic ethnic art. (Be careful with this one - adult supervision required.)
- Use the optional hands - on projects included in the appendix of this book for your Review Week ideas. Have fun with it!
- Take picture of what you did and tape/paste them in your Student Journal. (Send them to me, too! I would love to see what you've done.)

Tips for Teaching Struggling Learners

* Look through this book and Student's Journal and decide which material is the most important for your child to learn **permanently**. Before you even start the program with your children, write those chosen concepts on index cards and keep them in a safe place. As you go through the course, pull them out and use them to review with your child.

* Connect all new information to something familiar. It is easier for any of us to permanently remember something when we have something familiar to tie it to. Teach your children (all of them!) mnemonic devices. You know, "In 1492, Columbus sailed the Ocean blue…"

* Hands on activities! Most children remember better the more senses they use. Just hearing it is not enough for most of us; we need to write about it, see it, and create it!

* Review often! I have six reviews written into this course for you. Capitalize on them! Spend the entire week really getting into the story. Take time to plan meals, crafts, skits, and anything else you can think of that will cement the story for your children. All children benefit from review. (Adults do too!) The Reviews are in the Journal.

* Encouragement; something so simple but so profound. Words of encouragement are always remembered. Build up your children!

* If your child struggles with writing, be his scribe. I have been known to write neatly in a light colored, thin line highlighter as my child dictates what is on her mind. Afterward, she goes over it with a pencil making sure she forms her letters the correct way. Viola! Oral composition, history, and handwriting all in one!

* My son has a difficult time recalling particular information from a story, so to help him out, I write a list of information I want him to listen for as I read. To do

this, skim the section you are going to read to your children. Choose several key points, names, dates, or locations and write them on a piece of paper. Have them check it off as they hear you read it. They can also use their checklist to aid in oral narration later.

* For most children who struggle, repetition is the key. The more times they hear it, the more likely they will remember it. Don't be afraid to reread a chapter as a bed-time story. Or if your child can read on their own, let them re-read it. As they read, they can point out words they may not know. We have done some pretty heavy duty vocabulary building in this way!

* Show the child how the story relates to them. Talk about how they can apply it to themselves. Sometimes we think that a child is listening and applying, but when we actually talk to them about it, that particular character trait or flaw went right in one ear and out the other!

* Use the timeline project often to sequence the story. Telling and retelling builds confidence especially if they get to show off their work.

* Last, but most certainly <u>NOT</u> least, pray with your child. Teach your child to pray for understanding and the ability to learn. Let him see <u>you</u> praying for him.

Works Cited

[1] Chapter 4:
*Christian History Made Easy**, pg. 28, last paragraph

[2] Chapter 11:
Christian History Made Easy pg. 68 - 69

[3] Chapter 12:
Christian History Made Easy pg. 70

[4] Chapter 14:
Christian History Made Easy pg. 73, fifth paragraph

[5] Chapter 21:
Christian History Made Easy pg. 110, third paragraph

**Christian History Made Easy*
© 2009, by Timothy Paul Jones
Rose Publishing, Inc.
4733 Torrance Blvd. #259 Torrance, California 90503

Suggested Supplementary Reading

For Elementary Aged

"Castle Diary" by Richard Platt

"Peter the Great" by Diane Stanley

"Michelangelo" by Diane Stanley

"The Apprentice" by Pilar Molina LLorente

"The Adventures of Robin Hood" (Classic Starts) by Howard Pyle "The Minstrel in the Tower"

by Gloria Skurzynski

"Good Masters! Sweet Ladies!" by Laura Amy Schlitz

"Good Queen Bess" by Diane Stanley and Peter Vennema

For Jr. High and High School

"Adam of the Road" by Elizabeth Janet Gray

"The Samurai's Tale" by Erik Christian Haugaard "Black Horses for the King" Anne McCaffrey

"Son of Charlemagne" by Barbara Willard "Leonardo da Vinci" by Emily Hahn

"I, Juan de Pareja" by Elizabeth Barton de Trevino "The Shakespeare Stealer" by Gary

Blackwood "Master Cornhill" by Eloise Jarvis McGraw

"Mary, Bloody Mary" by Carolyn Meyer

"Catherine Called Birdy" by Karen Cushman

Movies

- Our all-time favorite Robin Hood movie is the 1950's version with Richard Todd staring as Robin.

- "The Quest for King Arthur" DVD put out by History Channel, is more of a look into the life and times of this legendary figure than it is a movie. (Please note: I have only seen parts of this. Please watch completely before allowing your children to see it!)

- PBS DVD - Castle - David Macaulay (This educational dvd combines animation and live action documentary to tell the story of a 13th century Welsh castle.) Recommended.

Made in the USA
Lexington, KY
28 July 2016